America's Spectacular
NORTHWEST

Photographed by Robert W. Madden

Prepared by the Special Publications Division
National Geographic Society, Washington, D. C.

Pinnacles of man and nature reach skyward, creating Seattle's distinctive cityscape. Flanked by mountains, embraced by waters of Puget Sound, the growing city sparkles in a 24-carat setting. New construction steadily reshapes the skyline. To the southeast rises Mount Rainier, a beacon to the wilderness that still claims much of the Northwest. PRECEDING PAGE: *A bull elk's bugling celebrates a Rocky Mountain morning in Montana.*
TOM AND PAT LEESON

AMERICA'S SPECTACULAR NORTHWEST

Photographed by ROBERT W. MADDEN

Contributing Authors: ROWE FINDLEY, ROBERT W.
MADDEN, MARK MILLER, CYNTHIA RUSS RAMSAY,
BILL RICHARDS

Published by
  The National Geographic Society
  GILBERT M. GROSVENOR, President
  MELVIN M. PAYNE, Chairman of the Board
  OWEN R. ANDERSON, Executive Vice President
  ROBERT L. BREEDEN, Vice President, Publications
    and Educational Media

Prepared by
  The Special Publications Division
  DONALD J. CRUMP, Editor
  PHILIP B. SILCOTT, Associate Editor
  WILLIAM L. ALLEN, WILLIAM R. GRAY, Senior Editors

Staff for this book
  SEYMOUR L. FISHBEIN, Managing Editor
  JOHN G. AGNONE, Picture Editor
  SUEZ B. KEHL, Art Director
  BARBARA L. GRAZZINI, Senior Researcher; RUTH L.
    CONNOR, SALLIE M. GREENWOOD, KATHERYN M.
    SLOCUM, Researchers

Illustrations and Design
  MARIANNE R. KOSZORUS, Assistant Art Director
  JANET DYER, D. RANDY YOUNG, Design Assistants
  JOHN D. GARST, JR., SUSANAH B. BROWN, GARY M.
    JOHNSON, SUSAN M. JOHNSTON, JUDITH BELL SIEGEL,
    ALFRED L. ZEBARTH, Map Research, Design,
    and Production
  WILLIAM P. BEAMAN, TONI EUGENE, KAREN M.
    KOSTYAL, CHRISTINE ECKSTROM LEE, LISA A. OLSON,
    KATHLEEN F. TETER, JENNIFER C. URQUHART,
    SUZANNE VENINO, Picture Legend Writers

Engraving, Printing, and Product Manufacture
  ROBERT W. MESSER, Manager
  GEORGE V. WHITE, Production Manager
  MARK R. DUNLEVY, Production Project Manager
  RICHARD A. McCLURE, RAJA D. MURSHED,
    CHRISTINE A. ROBERTS, DAVID V. SHOWERS,
    GREGORY STORER, Assistant Production Managers
  KATHERINE H. DONOHUE, Senior Production Assistant
  KATHERINE R. LEITCH, Production Staff Assistant

DEBRA A. ANTONINI, NANCY F. BERRY, PAMELA A. BLACK,
  NETTIE BURKE, JANE H. BUXTON, MARY ELIZABETH DAVIS,
  CLAIRE M. DOIG, ROSAMUND GARNER, VICTORIA D.
  GARRETT, MARY JANE GORE, JANE R. HALPIN, NANCY J.
  HARVEY, JOAN HURST, ARTEMIS S. LAMPATHAKIS,
  VIRGINIA A. McCOY, MERRICK P. MURDOCK, CLEO
  PETROFF, VICTORIA I. PISCOPO, TAMMY PRESLEY, CAROL
  A. ROCHELEAU, CATHERINE S. SILCOTT, KATHERYN M.
  SLOCUM, JENNY TAKACS, Staff Assistants

ANNE K. McCAIN, Index

PAUL CHESLEY

Realm of wondrous diversity, the Northwest
begins on the foggy, forested shores of the
Pacific Coast and spreads eastward high into
the meadows of the Rocky Mountains, where
chipmunks dine on cow parsnip seeds. Explorer
and naturalist John Muir marveled at such
panoplies, describing the fogs as "grand,
far-reaching affairs . . . the infinite delicacy . . .
of their touch as they linger to caress the tall
evergreens is most exquisite." On chipmunks:
"I never weary watching them . . . gathering
seeds and berries, like song sparrows posing
daintily on slender twigs."

Contents

Ways of the Old West swing with a woman's lasso at the Whitehorse Ranch in Oregon. Desert neighbors, men and women, pitch in at roundup time. Founded in 1869, the ranch soon won fame for elegant living; its owner rode a fine white horse caparisoned in silver.

Introduction

By Robert W. Madden

"WHERE WOULD YOU LIKE to live in the Northwest?" A Seattle resident asked me this question, presuming that I would consider living nowhere else. I heard many similar expressions implying unabashed love for this magnificent land during the year I spent roving the cities and back roads of Washington, Oregon, Idaho, and that portion of Montana west of the Great Divide.

Rich Davis expressed it one raw spring day as we shared lunch over the wide, flat hood of a four-wheel-drive pickup in eastern Oregon's high desert country. On horseback since dawn, Rich had been driving range cattle toward massive Steens Mountain and summer grazing.

"When I got out of the service in Germany, I toured Europe with a rodeo. But I grew up in the Harney Basin and I began to miss these wide open spaces," he said. Rich exchanged waves with a ten-gallon silhouette in a passing pickup.

"I know most everybody here," he said, "and more important, they know me."

The Northwest presents a panoply of climes and geography. I skied the trackless powder of Idaho's Sawtooths; I watched dust devils swirl over treeless wheat fields in eastern Washington; I hiked a rain-soaked trail to Cloudy Pass in the North Cascades; I listened to Pacific breakers thundering against the cliffs as I stood at Cape Foulweather.

Diverse land, diverse people. In Eugene, Oregon, I met a logger who despised government bureaucracy in forest management, and a teacher who lobbied for tougher environmental laws. Both loved the land.

I was raised in America's breadbasket, that seemingly endless expanse of cultivated fields in the Midwest. My profession of photojournalism took me to the populated Northeast, where true wilderness is rare. It was with this background that I witnessed the North-

west's spectacular panoramas and experienced a land as natural and pristine as the one our forefathers saw.

This is a young land in a young country. Brief visits here by sea were made by James Cook in 1778 and by George Vancouver in 1792, but it was the Lewis and Clark exploration in 1805-06 that foreshadowed the development of an overland trail. Spurred on by talk of good land and great riches, pioneers trekked to the fabled Oregon country, many over the arduous Oregon Trail. Portland was incorporated in 1851; Seattle was settled about then. Today the entire population of the Northwest—some 8.4 million—tops that of New York City by little more than a million.

More than half of all Northwesterners live in the lush zone between the ocean and the Cascade Range. This region includes the "I-5" corridor, named for Interstate 5, the main north-south artery.

Commerce centers on the two largest cities in the corridor, Seattle and Portland, whose historic rivalry seems to have abated. Today the vibrant metropolis of Seattle looks to Denver and San Francisco for comparisons, whereas Portland seems to strive for livability rather than big-city status.

Irresistible scenery flanks the corridor and plays an important role in urban lifestyles. To the west beckon the surf, the craggy coastline, and the inland sea sprinkled with agreeable islands. On the eastern horizon the mist-shrouded Cascades, cloaked with tall conifers and crowned by snowcapped summits, form a majestic backdrop.

While scudding Pacific storms give the Northwest its rain—and rainy reputation—they rarely get by the Cascades crests, leaving much of the Northwest semiarid. The peaks are not only a precipitation barrier, but a social barrier as well. East of the mountains the land of western dress begins. Cowboy hats,

Majesty of the Olympic Mountains enfolds a solitary figure skirting a glacial crevasse on 6,809-foot-high Snow Dome. Nearly half the Northwest's acreage lies in federal ownership—parks, forests, wildlife refuges, public lands. On some, cattle graze and loggers fell trees. Preservationists often seek to keep them untrammeled. In unspoiled places such as Olympic National Park, the nation harvests inexhaustible delight.

boots, and rodeos are as much a part of life here as are cosmopolitan restaurants and fashionable shops a part of Seattle.

In the northern Rockies a frontier attitude of independence exists. Often, I found the attitude more difficult to pursue than to dream. To pry a living from these mountains, some try mining, some trap, others log or cater to tourists. In a small mining town with memories of better times, I asked an old-timer what folks did for a living.

"Nowadays they rub two tourists together for three months of the year," he snorted, "and for the other nine months they wait for 'em to come back."

Few tourists take the long gravel road to Fields, Oregon (population 10). Fewer still drive another 35 miles to the Whitehorse Ranch, a historic spread in the Alvord basin of the Oregon desert. I did one day, with ranch manager Harry House, the pickup bouncing along a treeless expanse stretching to the horizon. The ranch spreads across half a million acres—give or take an acre, said Harry. For more specific information he referred me to the Whitehorse Ranch, Inc., on Wilshire Boulevard in Beverly Hills, California.

When large spreads are sold, rising land prices sometimes overshadow the financial condition of the working ranch. Most locals can't afford to buy, but for those who sell their ranches, it can be a bonanza. "These ranch owners work poor and die rich," said county extension agent Paul Friedrichsen.

Most of the land in the Northwest, however, is not privately owned. More than 60 percent is under the stewardship of the United States Forest Service, the Bureau of Land Management, and other federal and state agencies. They have had difficulty satisfying the demands on these lands by loggers, miners, ranchers, environmentalists, and other interest groups. "Land of Many Uses," proclaim

9

wooden signs at the entrance of many of the national forests. "Land of many abuses," claims a Seattle-based environmentalist, unhappy with Forest Service management.

Another view. Flying over the French Pete Wilderness in the southern Cascades, pilot Herb Henderson tipped our helicopter slightly and pointed into the valley. His voice came flat over the intercom.

"See all those dead trees? They're just dying from old age, and nobody can get in to log them. What a waste."

Scenes of logging crews dragging 300-year-old behemoths from virgin forests exist on postcards but are no longer a part of 20th-century logging. Now timber companies are developing trees which mature in 40 to 60 years and are grown in rows on tree farms.

The mighty Columbia River now runs deep and silent over its legendary rapids, dammed for flood control and electricity. In 1883, 43 million pounds of Chinook salmon were caught in the lower Columbia. Today, at Clifton, Oregon, where fishermen spin yarns and mend nets, they speak with pride of their latest fishing adventures—in Alaska. Commercial fishing here is fast becoming a part of history. In 1980 the Chinook season was a mere 14 days; the catch, 1.2 million pounds.

The fishermen distribute blame for the situation among Indians, loggers, dams, hatcheries, sport fishermen, and the government. Actually, the increase in population with all its ramifications, combined with sophisticated fishing technology, has put tremendous pressure on salmon runs.

The region's population grows at twice the national rate. Cities swell; skyscrapers multiply. Yet a feeling of the frontier remains. I sensed it across the land—in silent desert pungent with sage, in the taste of a mountain stream, fresh as sunrise. So the Northwest weaves its spell. May it never be broken.

America's grand northwest corner blends a rich mosaic of life and landscape: Puget Sound, pulsing with freighters and ferries and pleasure fleets of sail . . . the long sliver of coast, busied by timber and fishing ports and raucous resorts . . . the Cascades, innards of fire, crowns of ice . . . eastern Oregon and southern Idaho, high and dry, homes on the range few—and far between . . . farmlands, from Willamette and the orchard valleys, Yakima and Wenatchee, to the Palouse Hills, amber waves of grain . . . the Columbia, workaholic river, powering factories, slaking scrubland . . . the Rockies barrier, athrob with mining fever, dotted with lonely hamlets and sanctuaries filled with the wonder of wild things.

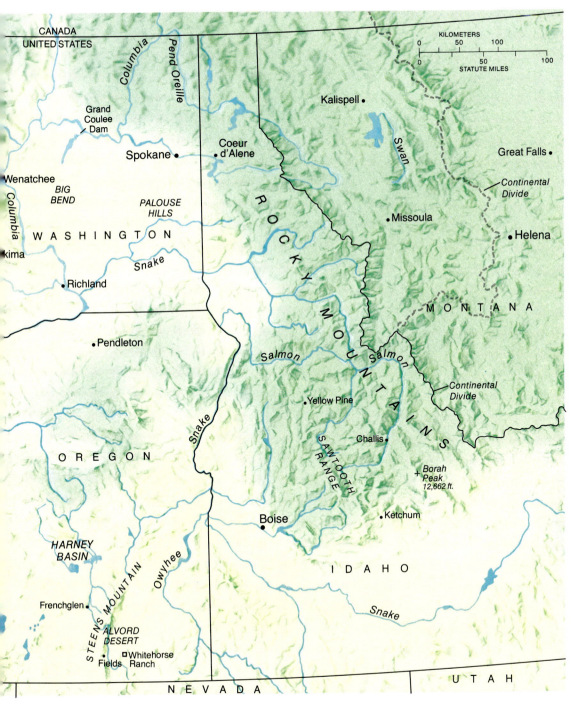

The San Juans, once called a "cluster of mountain tops sticking up out of the sea," comprise 172 evergreen islands—some bustling, some wild, a few inaccessible—along the northern edge of Puget Sound. State ferries, such as this one, provide mass transit across these waters.

Puget Sound

By Cynthia Russ Ramsay

The wind moaned in the rigging. Short, steep waves shattered into spray on the lee rail as *Night Runner* slashed across the choppy waters of Puget Sound in the cold November rain. We had rounded the halfway mark in the annual Hat Island Race from Seattle, when a squall charged up out of the south, bringing gusts up to 40 knots that heeled the 42-foot cutter over hard.

"The wind's up. We've got to shorten sail," shouted the skipper, Douglas Fryer, over the howl of the gale. "Strike the number one jib and set the number two. And let's tie another reef in the mainsail." The seven-man crew, bulky figures in bright yellow rain gear, wrestled with sail on a slanting deck awash with foaming sea. Doug, a Seattle attorney and celebrated yachtsman, turned the wheel a scant two spokes, heading just enough into the wind to ease the strain on the rig.

A novice among seasoned sailors, I sat wonderfully idle at the stern and out of the way, my eyes drawn to the matchless landscape that enfolds Puget Sound. I looked across the scowling sea toward the evergreen stillness of the shores. Gulls perched on a set of old pilings; boats bobbed at their moorings in front of a scattering of houses; ahead, the white-and-green hulk of a commuter ferry trailed a frothy wake across the dark water.

In the western distance cottony clouds draped the jagged crests of the Olympic Mountains and spilled down the rumpled, timbered flanks in tendrils of mist. To the east, beyond a fringe of flat farmland, were the snowy heights of the Cascades, invisible behind a wall of low clouds.

Between these two bold and beautiful ranges lies Puget Sound—a saltwater basin whose great depths had been scoured by glaciers that melted 14,000 years ago. As the ice receded, the Pacific flowed in through the Strait of Juan de Fuca, spreading east and south for 180 miles, filling the lowlands. This arm of the sea thrusts into vast forests of giant evergreens that have created fortunes for the timber barons of the Northwest.

Though bracketed by land, Puget Sound seethes with ocean tides, back eddies, tricky currents, and, at times, with capricious winds that veer off the islands and the heavily indented shore. The constantly changing conditions completely absorbed Doug in steering his boat—a lovely, luxurious craft of molded wood. He had been at the helm for hours, muscles tensed, when he turned toward me and said, "Nothing compares with the feeling of freedom I find in sailing."

At midpoint in the 42-mile race, with only one boat ahead, Doug took a calculated risk. He split from the fleet of some 170 boats and changed course to run down the west side of the channel. But the southwest wind he had gambled on came too late.

"It's terrific to win," said Doug, "but it's not devastating to lose. Either way, I can't ever get enough of sailing."

Boating, whether under sail or in an outboard or a twin-engine cruiser, is a way of life here. One in every five Puget Sound families owns some kind of pleasure craft. And on a summer weekend, when the hum of motors drifts across the waters and sailboats cluster like pale petals offshore, it seems half the population is afloat.

Nearly three million people, three out of every four Washingtonians, live in Puget Sound country—on the islands and along the bays and channels that create more than 2,000 twisting miles of shoreline.

For several weeks I traveled across this realm of deep forests, broad valleys, and busy ports. Day after glistening day I savored the serene beauty of the San Juan Islands just north of the sound proper. I watched rose sunsets fade into night behind the jagged

Mapping the region in 1792, British Capt. George Vancouver named inlets south of Tacoma for Lt. Peter Puget, who explored them. Today the name covers the length of this arm of the Pacific; the sound spans some 80 miles, but its contorted coastline has as many miles as does the coast from Canada to southern California. The strait to the sea honors the Greek seaman Apostolos Valerianos, who claimed to have seen it in 1592. History finds little support for the claim, but the honors remain: Valerianos sailed for the Spaniards, who called him Juan de Fuca. Seattle, an infant lumber port in mid-19th century, crowns a growing urban empire of industry and international trade.

silhouette of booming Seattle, its skyline bristling with glass office towers and high-rise hotels—all built since 1968.

I watched sleek black-and-white killer whales dive beneath the waters near Friday Harbor and nuclear submarines rise to the surface near the navy yard in Bremerton. I heard the screech of bald eagles, the whine of sawmills, and the hollow boom of foghorns in the night. I wandered fields where acres and acres of tulips and daffodils shine with color; and I gazed with pure pleasure at the snowy, barren splendor of Mount Rainier, majestic and alone, floating like a lovely shimmering dream above the far horizon. I shopped for pottery at Uwajimaya's, a Japanese supermarket-department store, and I sipped Washington champagne in a French chateau that is home to the Ste. Michelle Winery. Before long it became perfectly clear why nearly a million people have flocked to the Puget Sound region in the past 20 years.

More than 400 new firms have located in the area since 1970, and the eminently livable cities and the opportunities for outdoor recreation help the big companies recruit the skills they need. "Where else are the outdoors so marvelously accessible to an urban area?" one personnel director asked me. "Where else can you leave a factory and go fishing or for a sail after work?"

Then he handed me a full-page want ad for computer specialists that cited Seattle's numerous theaters, restaurants, and art galleries. The ad also told of the 2,500 miles of ocean beaches, the 2,000 miles of hiking trails, and the more than 90 species of sport fishes in nearby waters. The industries and cities are concentrated along the sound's eastern perimeter—along Interstate 5, connecting Olympia, the state capital, Tacoma, Seattle, and Everett, and Bellingham near the Canadian border. *(Continued on page 21)*

The ghost of a company town on San Juan Island finds new life as a boaters' resort. "Largest lime works in the west," boasted Roche Harbor early in this century. Amid kilns and quarries, the company owner, whose home has become a restaurant (below), lived in princely style; guests enjoyed salmon barbecues and dances on a tree-lined barge floating by splendid sunset scenes—scenes that still grace the harbor (right). A historical park on the island commemorates an Anglo-American dispute over claims to the archipelago. The Pig War—named for its only casualty—brought troops from both sides. Capt. George Pickett built the American earthwork here, a few years before his charge at Gettysburg. The U. S. won the islands in arbitration.

Sixty-five feet longer than the Wright brothers' first flight, a 185-foot Boeing 747 wheels toward the paint hangar from final assembly in the Everett plant—the largest building in the world by volume. Boeing has claimed world leadership among commercial jet makers since 1954, when it rolled out the 707 prototype. By the time the wide-body 747 arrived in 1968, the Boeing family of jetliners had grown to four. In 1981 a new member of the family

made its debut—the twin-engine, medium-range 767 (below, left). Designers aimed for a "plane of the future," with lower engine noise levels and more efficient fuel consumption. Before the ceremonial rollout of the first 767, its maker had firm orders for 173, options for another 138, with passenger flights scheduled to begin in late 1982. Boeing ranks as Puget Sound's largest employer and the nation's leading manufacturer in dollar value of exports.

Seattle developer Martin Selig set the bold slants of the building behind him to capture the energy of sunlight, coming and going. Though plans for the solar panels fell through, the builders kept the rooflines. In a courtyard below, a laid-back benchwarmer, cast in bronze, and a lounger take in the morning sun. New office towers, hotels, and condominiums rise swiftly on Seattle's skyline. Selig holds blueprints for the 76-story Columbia Center, planned as the tallest skyscraper in the West Coast states.

A nearly continuous chain of suburbs, subdivisions, and gleaming shopping malls links the cities into a 150-mile metropolitan corridor that has been dubbed Pugetopolis.

The highway cuts through a misty region of shipyards and deepwater ports, electronics and food-processing plants, military bases, and giant pulp and paper mills whose stacks send billowing plumes to the sky. But the biggest single economic force in the area is the Boeing Company—the western world's largest aircraft manufacturer, builder of jets, missiles, computers, and space hardware, and employer of some 75,000 people here.

Its founder, the late William E. Boeing, constructed his first plane of piano wire, spruce lumber, and linen in 1916. Since then, his company has built a reputation as one of the world's best plane makers. But a little over a decade ago, with a drop in demand for 747s and the nation turning away from the supersonic transport, Boeing

endured some difficult years. The company cut its work force in the Seattle area by 64,000; the slump gave rise to a gallows humor saying that went, "Will the last person to leave Seattle turn off the lights." In fact, few left—a small fraction of the unemployed.

Now business for Boeing is better than ever, I was told, and inside the 61.8-acre, 11-story plant in Everett—the world's largest building in volume—workers assemble a 747 every six days. The harsh staccato of riveting blended into one muted snarl as I walked the great length of the building. Overhead, a crane system running on ceiling tracks moved the nose to the fuselage and parts of the tail through assembly. In the paint hangar I watched the 16 men who work for three days to spray the jumbo with 600 pounds of paint.

It was no quieter at the plant at Renton, 40 miles to the south, where Boeing has designed a brand-new generation of planes— the 767 and 757, the first new American commercial aircraft in more than a decade.

"Until the energy crunch came, Boeing designed planes for speed. Now the premium is on fuel efficiency," explained John Wheeler of Boeing's Commercial Airplane Company. We paused before a full-scale mock-up of the wide-body 767, which uses 35 percent less fuel than the midsize planes it was designed to replace—a potential savings of 80,000 gallons of fuel a year for each aircraft.

From the drawing boards and laboratories of Boeing have come many of the designs for the rockets that helped land astronauts on the moon and for spacecraft that launched unmanned missions to the planets. At a research center in a Seattle suburb, I found Boeing's wizards of high technology working on a space station design and devising a system to capture solar energy in space and beam it to receiver antennas on earth.

A less dramatic but no less significant search for knowledge goes on nearby at giant Weyerhaeuser, which grows and harvests timber on nearly six million acres of forest lands in the United States, and manufactures a multitude of wood products ranging from plywood and paper to milk cartons and diapers. At headquarters north of Tacoma, company scientists seek to grow wood better than nature alone could do it. Ever since the nation's first tree farm was established on Weyerhaeuser land in 1941, the main objective has been to produce more wood per acre with faster growing, better quality trees and more efficient techniques in forest and mill. The energy crisis has also triggered research on ways to use the limbs, stumps, and needles left over in a clear-cut forest.

Technology has also transformed shavings and sawdust into particle board, bark into ground cover, and lignin, a residue of pulp production and useful as fuel, into a vanilla substitute.

No such innovations were deemed necessary at the turn of the century, an era of cut-and-run logging when progress was measured in the number of stumps left behind. In those years the booming lumber industry accounted for a majority of the wage earners in all of Washington State.

Teams of oxen dragged, or skidded, the great trees to the mills along roads made of logs laid crosswise to the route. These wooden skids also became the road to town, where loggers brawled and gambled and caroused after months of work in the woods.

Along Seattle's Skid Road, vice was so rampant that in the 1880s revenues from the merchants of sin provided 50 percent of the city's budget. In time, the district deteriorated and the term Skid Road, or Skid Row, came to signify a place where out-of-luck, forgotten folk huddle in doorways and sleep on benches or in flophouses. But in the 1960s, the decayed buildings, saloons, and gambling joints were stylishly renovated, and the area enjoyed an unaccustomed respectability.

The sun had burned away the morning fog, and Mount Rainier had once again emerged as a glorious white presence in the distant sky, when I arrived for a stroll in Pioneer Square—heart of wicked old Seattle.

Today the streets around Pioneer Square present a new hazard. The Victorian brick buildings, which went up after a great fire in 1889, now house antique shops, art galleries, craft studios, bookstores, and chic boutiques that present an almost irresistible temptation.

Exhausted from the effort of shopping without spending, I consoled myself with lunch at the Brasserie Pittsbourg, one of several fine restaurants in the vicinity. Unpretentious, with white butcher paper covering the tables, and utterly Gallic, with the scent of herbs in the air, the restaurant embodies the strong views of its director, Saigon-born,

"It's like being on vacation year round," says a resident of the neighborhood floating on Lake Union. Floating homes in the middle of Seattle date to the 19th century. Unlike houseboats, these stay put—at locations that can be leased or bought, with sewer hookups. Some moorages have gone condominium; a single one may cost $150,000. FOLLOWING PAGES: The priceless view from Lake Union. Built for the 1962 World's Fair, Seattle's famed Space Needle rises 607 feet; near its top a restaurant slowly revolves.

Paris-trained François Kissel: "Begin with good bread, good butter, and good soup. Buy only the natural, freshest ingredients available locally."

Few cities in the world offer such lively access to fresh produce as Pike Place Market. The cries of vendors and the hand-lettered signs on paper bags promise cucumbers picked yesterday, tomatoes ripened on the vine, and salmon straight from the sea.

Pasqualina Verdi, one of the 50 or so truck farmers who sell produce at the tables inside the long main arcade, sometimes complains, "Everybody look, nobody cook."

The tourists mill about and admire the fruits and vegetables, washed and gleaming, the iced trays of salmon, trout, and red snapper, and the orderly rows of Dungeness crabs, their front claws bound with red rubber bands. Locals do most of the food buying, and locals as well as tourists shop the stalls where craftspeople display jewelry, belts, pottery, stained glass, and paintings.

It was hard to imagine that this bustling mart almost fell before the wrecker's ball. An urban renewal plan threatened to replace it with offices, apartments, and a parking garage. The people themselves saved the market—voting against the original plan and in favor of making the area a historical district.

The city, I discovered, has always had an aggressive "can-do" attitude, an activism referred to as the Seattle Spirit. As one transplant from Boston told me, "Seattle is a bootstrap town. People don't realize some things can't be done, so they simply go ahead and do them."

In the 1870s every town on Puget Sound was competing for the railroads. When Seattle lost out to *(Continued on page 28)*

"Sailing ships," wrote chronicler of sail Alan Villiers, "have always raced; while two survive, they always will." Nowhere truer than on Puget Sound. Most races on these waters take place in spring and autumn, when the breezes pick up and blow strong enough to swell out the spinnakers (above). Explorer Scout Katie Gosanko jibes the mainsail of Heather (left), a 41-foot sloop on which teenagers learn the ropes. One lesson: Avoid a snakepit of lines like the one below. The team sweater (below, left) builds esprit. In most races the scouts finish well back, but in 1981 they swept to victory in a 136-mile race, beating—among others—the benefactor who donated Heather to scouting, John Buchan, a top-ranked sailor of the Northwest.

Catch of the day, a sockeye salmon passes between workers at Pike Place Market, a triumph of preservation near Seattle's waterfront. Since the early 1900s fishermen and farmers have brought their fresh foods here. In recent decades, as new shopping centers siphoned trade, a move arose to raze the old market. The voters saved it. Pike Place thrives anew; fish, produce, groceries, crafts, street musicians—the "soul of Seattle."

Tacoma as the terminus for the Northern Pacific, indignant Seattleites refused to be eclipsed. Business leaders raised the funds, and able-bodied men hoisted pickaxes and shovels and began to build their own set of tracks. Their efforts failed, but eventually the city was served by two railroads.

Citizens also lobbied relentlessly in the territorial legislature until Seattle was chosen as the site of the University of Washington. Now a major research institution with a preeminent health sciences center, the University has pioneered in the techniques for bone marrow transplants, the treatment of pain, and improvements in kidney dialysis.

In 1897 the Chamber of Commerce boldly seized the Alaska gold rush trade with a clever publicity campaign that linked Seattle with Alaska and the gold in the Klondike. Soon the city swarmed with thousands of stampeders. "The gold rush boom and the monopoly of Alaska trade, plus the new trade with Japan, made this city the commercial hub of the Northwest," explained Fred Short, a spokesman for the Port of Seattle, as he led me along the waterfront where more than 2,200 oceangoing vessels call each year.

Acres of Japanese Datsuns created a shiny landscape of color beside the massive silos that in 1980 funneled more than three million tons of American grain into ships. Farther south stood giant, high-speed cranes, part of the farsighted investment in facilities that has made Seattle one of the country's largest ports for containerized shipping—vying with Oakland as the West Coast leader.

The port on Elliott Bay—with its parade of containerships, freighters, tugs, barges, and ferries that can swallow all the cars in a large parking lot—comprises only a part of Seattle's marvelously varied waterfront.

Handsome homes, set amid manicured lawns notched with private docks, rise along the broad curve of Lake Washington, which marks the city's eastern limits and separates it from such comfortable suburbs as Bellevue, Kirkland, and Mercer Island. On smaller Lake Union some 470 floating homes line the shore. Some are lavish architectural cubes in weathered cedar and glass; a few are ramshackle sheds. All enjoy ducklings at their doorsteps and the languor of rocking ever so gently on placid waters. The two lakes are connected to Puget Sound by the Washington Ship Canal, which winds for eight miles just north of downtown. Near the canal locks that lead to tidewater sits the Fishermen's Terminal. The men who moor their vessels here lead a rugged life, filled with uncertainty, demanding constant vigilance.

In Seattle and at other fishing ports such as Port Townsend, Anacortes, and Bellingham, I talked with these men—and a few women as well—who walk a pitching deck sometimes numb with cold, sometimes wet and weary, but ever hopeful. There were gillnetters, who fish at night so the salmon won't see the entangling webs, and purse seiners, who on good days trap tons of fish in their huge encircling nets. Others troll for salmon, haul pots for crab, and long-line for halibut. They were all outspoken free spirits.

And they were saddened, as I was, by the death of Philip Sutherland, one of the most outspoken among them, in the fall of 1981. His boat capsized in a gale, and he was lost, after 32 years of gillnetting. I had met him a year earlier; we talked of the days when "all the fisherman had was a steering wheel

and a boat that moved. We used a lot more muscle then." Now motors pull the catch aboard. Still, Phil felt that regulation had made salmon fishing tougher than ever.

To manage the stocks of Chinook, coho, sockeye, and chum salmon, which have

"Bernie Gobin drew a deep breath before he spoke for his people—some 1,300 Tulalip Indians whose reservation lies just north of Everett. 'We were guaranteed those fishing rights by . . . treaties with the federal government,' he said, as we stood near the rough-hewn longhouse where the tribe gathers for ceremonies."

been in a declining trend for years, the Washington Department of Fisheries has divided Puget Sound and the Strait of Juan de Fuca into 31 districts for some 1,500 gillnetters and 360 purse seiners licensed to fish there. Each district has a separate catch quota in an effort to ensure that enough salmon reach their home streams to spawn.

"We never know which area will be open until it's put on the gillnetters hotline," Phil told me. "Then the whole fleet converges into that one shoebox, using expensive fuel to reach the open fishing grounds. After a night, or two at the most, the district is closed, and we wait around until the Indians have caught their share."

Phil, like other non-Indian fishermen, bitterly opposed the court decisions of the 1970s which decree that Indians are entitled to half the harvestable salmon passing through their tribal fishing areas. On the other hand the tribes on Puget Sound feel that an old injustice has been mitigated.

Bernie Gobin drew a deep breath before he spoke for his people—some 1,300 Tulalip Indians whose reservation lies just north of

Everett. "We were guaranteed those fishing rights by 19th-century treaties with the federal government," he said, as we stood near the rough-hewn longhouse where the tribe gathers for ceremonies and communal feasts. "In return for giving up titles to their lands, the Indians were to share the fishery *in common*. Every court has interpreted that as meaning the Indians share equally.

"The real problem is that there's too much effort for too little fish. Too many licenses have been granted to non-Indian fishermen, and the construction of dams and the pollution of streams have destroyed too many spawning grounds."

While Indian, federal, and state hatcheries seek to build up the salmon runs, others contend with what they see as another population problem—the rapid growth of Seattle and the rest of King County. From his column in the *Seattle Post-Intelligencer* Emmett Watson gleefully encourages his "dear, loyal constituents of Lesser Seattle to do battle against the nitwits praising the city." Some locals dwell on the soggy weather to dissuade people from moving in. They neglect to mention the pleasant summers and the winters that are sometimes so mild that roses are still abloom on New Year's. Precipitation in Seattle actually averages 39 inches a year—less than New York City's 40 inches. The rains here, however, tend to be lighter, so that winter brings many dour, drizzly days.

No one has fought longer or harder to combat Seattle's growing pains and the consequences of runaway development than lawyer James R. Ellis. A tireless crusader, he has labored for nearly 30 years to make Seattle a "humane city that people will love."

"There's no way we can halt growth. We can't put barbwire fences at the borders, but at the same time we need not allow rampant urban sprawl to smother the open space and beauty that has made this area so tremendously appealing," Ellis told me in his office 20 stories above Seattle's downtown core. From the big windows I could see a vista of construction cranes and the steel girders of skyscrapers on the way up. Seattle's building boom seemed to be little affected by a locally depressed lumber market; on the streets below, business was also brisk in the department stores and shops.

The activity was in sharp contrast to Tacoma's downtown, which seemed to me half empty by day and deserted at night. A smoke-stack city and an important port, Tacoma builds ships, refines copper, and turns out lumber, paper, and chemicals. Its resident population is over 100,000, but the executives and work force seem to prefer to shop in the Tacoma suburbs and tend to look to Seattle for their night on the town. Little wonder. On a November evening in Seattle I could choose from 20 plays, 4 concerts, and a lavish production of the opera *Aida*.

"For a long time Seattleites were self-conscious about the lack of culture in town, but we don't have to apologize any more," said Hal Calbom, a tall, curly haired, local TV reporter. We were in the revolving restaurant at the top of the Space Needle, Seattle's famous landmark. The panorama of the city slowly unfolded as Hal told me of the results of a market survey comparing Seattle with 19 other major cities: "Seattleites have more money than people in other cities and spend it faster. A lot of money goes on the road. We Seattleites drive more miles, each of us, than even the Californians do. Of the country's 20 biggest populations, we are per capita the number one buyers of books. We also rank first in the purchase of TV dinners. Perhaps as a result, Seattle leads the nation in going out to eat. The Seattle man ranks dead last in the purchase of suits. On the other hand, he leads in buying work boots, blue jeans, backpack equipment, and electric saws."

As we talked, the light was fading from the sky, and like the hundreds of commuters from Bainbridge Island, I cut short what I was doing to catch the ferry. I rode home with a young banker, Ned Palmer, standing on the deck, silent in the violet dusk. The rippling waters were stained red with the splendor of

"Gulls dipped and wheeled ...
as the ferry eased into its slip
in Friday Harbor, the largest town in
the San Juans. The ... run from Anacortes
had transported me into a unique world,
where a mosaic of 172 islands turns
every horizon into an enchanting
landscape of woodland, sea, and sky."

the dying sun, and the craggy peaks of the Olympics loomed as dark specters against a sky first rose then lilac.

Finally Ned, who had once worked on Wall Street in New York, spoke. "You can see why going home is no longer a frustrating experience. I can walk the deck, feel the wind, and find a little tranquillity watching the sunset, and in half an hour, when I get off on the other side, I am in the country."

Bainbridge Island—with homes, golf courses, and tennis courts amid the woodlands—is not quite rural, but Vashon Island, which lies to the south and requires a more inconvenient commute to the city, does retain a comfortable, rustic charm. For example, the 245-acre Wax Orchards on the island has not been carved up by developers, and Bob and Betsy Sestrap still raise what they call "cider bushes."

"We pick apples when they're so ripe they squirt in your eye when you bite into them," says Bob. "Then it's just a matter of crushing the apples and freezing the mash, so

we can produce cider year round." Many on Vashon also grow vegetables. But in years past emissions from the American Smelting and Refining Company copper smelter in Tacoma have contaminated the soils in the southernmost part of the island with traces of cadmium. As a result the local health department has cautioned those gardeners to avoid homegrown leafy vegetables.

Pollution also plagues the waters of Puget Sound. Scientists have recently detected a variety of pollutants, including PCBs and toxic metals in samples of bottom sediments, along with a disturbing incidence of diseases in bottom-dwelling shrimps, crabs, and fishes. The people involved in the National Oceanic and Atmospheric Administration study, however, feel more work is needed to determine how serious the problem is.

In addition, increasing deliveries of crude oil to the four refineries near Cherry Point and Anacortes, north of Seattle, bring increasing risks of oil spills. To reach those refineries, 107 miles from the open Pacific, tankers must nose through a maze of the hauntingly beautiful San Juan Islands, navigating winding channels sometimes barely a mile wide.

Gulls dipped and wheeled between sailboat masts as the ferry eased into its slip in Friday Harbor, the largest town in the San Juans. The two-and-a-half-hour run from Anacortes had transported me into a unique world, where a mosaic of 172 islands turns every horizon into an enchanting landscape of woodland, sea, and sky.

You have to drive up a mountain road near Friday Harbor to reach Tim and Cindy DeLapp's cabin on Eagle Crest. The noise of hammering told me I had arrived, for Tim is a carpenter who loves his work. He calls himself a tinkerer who doesn't like to depend on anyone, not even the utility companies.

Back in the pink, the Starrett House exemplifies the wave of restoration that has revived Port Townsend, rich in Victorian and Queen Anne houses. A failed bid for a railroad transformed the booming 19th-century port into the "world's only lighted cemetery." The Starrett House, built as a carpenter's showcase in 1889, became a funeral parlor and later a front for a bootlegger who used the hearse and coffins to transport illegal spirits. Its elegance restored, the house lives on as an inn.

"Our water comes off the galvanized iron roof into a water tank. We get our water from the sky, heat from the woods, and electricity from the wind," said Tim, a wiry 28-year-old with red hair and a bright smile.

A small steel tower supports his windmill, which provides electricity in winter, when a steady south wind blows. Tim is also building a steam engine as a backup generator during summer's calm.

Not everyone on the islands lives quite as economically. People pay $100,000 an acre just for beachfront land. "But it's got a million-dollar view, and you don't have to buy the water," says realtor Sam Buck.

Like many places in the Northwest, the islands confront growth and change. Tourists jam the ferries in summer. Surveyors' stakes pop up everywhere, like mushrooms after a rain. Newcomers speak fervently of tranquil beauty—of hillsides ablaze with California poppies, of great blue herons gliding above the water, of deer that stand at windows and wild turkeys that strut across the roads, of secluded coves where the only sound is the murmur of waves against the shore.

David Richardson of Orcas Island, a third-generation islander, feels there are a lot of things about the good old days he's glad to see go. "Except for businessmen and rich retirees, people mostly farmed or fished and were quite poor. Nowadays it's much easier to make a living in real estate, construction, or tourism. So more and more of us depend on growth, and are committed to growth."

To help preserve the rural character of the islands, the residents have adopted a land-use plan that, among other things, limits house lots in many places to a minimum of five acres. "What that also does is to reserve the islands for the rich," sighed Dave.

The hundred or so people on Waldron have resorted to more stringent measures to preserve their island and their life-style. No ferry stops; there are no shops or restaurants or telephones. Donna Ward told me that her family uses kerosene for light and hauls water from wells. "We grow all we can ourselves," she added, "and cook on a wood stove. We make cheese and corn-silk tea, and wine from rose petals, nettles, or blackberries."

I continued my amble along a road spangled by sunshine and shadow beneath its leafy canopy of trees. I passed the schoolhouse where an MD conducts kindergarten, and Peter Alexander, a scientist, teaches math. School was out and I found Peter in a large clearing helping a neighbor repair a roof in exchange for firewood. He jumped down when I hailed him, and as we sat with the sun warm on our backs, he explained why he finds his new way of life so satisfying.

"Each person here feels that he does make a difference. I never before felt so attached to a place; perhaps it's the hands-on physical life-style. Yet I'm not that sure we spend all that much time in the mechanics of living, for my family seems to have more time to enjoy each other's company. Added to all that, there's the comfort and satisfaction of living in a close-knit community where people share their skills."

At 36, Peter finds pleasure and a deep satisfaction in his new life. From all across the country, Americans have come to Puget Sound, to its beauty as well as to its economic opportunity. They have come to raise oysters in Quilcene on the verdant shores of the Hood Canal; to run a Victorian mansion in picturesque Port Townsend as a gracious inn; to teach at the universities in Bellingham, Tacoma, and Seattle. There are retirees, and young executives on the way up. Will the region succeed in retaining its beauty? Just, maybe. But it is hard to imagine the lands of Puget Sound will ever be like anyplace else.

Nooksack Indians turn to technology to preserve a traditional fishery. At the mouth of the Nooksack River they net Chinook salmon, place transmitters (far left) in their stomachs, and release them. A flying biologist (left) tracks the signals to the spawning ground. From there, some of the salmon go to a hatchery pond (below). Workers strip the eggs (right)—as many as 5,000 from one female—and propagate them. A year later they release the fry; one in a hundred will make it back.

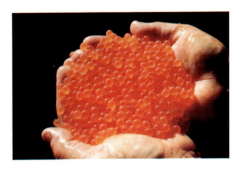

The technique of reef netting: As sockeye salmon migrate from the Pacific to the Fraser River in Canada, towed barges take position off Lummi Island (right). Each pair sets a net to form a sloping underwater barrier between the two. Buoyed lines, strung with plastic seaweed to resemble reefs, widen out from the boats to funnel approaching salmon. On the boat towers spotters peer down through Polaroid sunglasses (below). When a school reaches the net, a spotter shouts; winches swiftly hoist the catch, and flailing sockeyes come aboard. Indian canoes with hand-hauled nets of willow bark once caught salmon this way.

Summer calm in the ocean's assault on the Oregon coast leaves cliffsides and sea stacks standing defiantly at Bandon—for the moment. Winter storms dramatically whittle away the Northwest's shore, and fog drifts in and out in all seasons, as if inspecting the action.

The Coast

By Cynthia Russ Ramsay

*E*verywhere along the green and hilly Northwest coast, fog blows in from the ocean and drifts across the land like a whispered benediction. Sometimes the fog is so thick that the steep headlands jutting into the Pacific, the pastures dotted with dairy herds, and the wooded hills webbed with logging roads disappear from sight. Sometimes only a soft mist rises from the sea, and then the giant trees in the moss-hung Olympic rain forests, the row upon row of fishing boats idling in ports, and the clam diggers on the crescent beaches loom like ghostly silhouettes in the feeble light.

Some days fog lingers in patches, and when the black, long-necked cormorants swoop off their rocky roosts, they fly into and out of obscurity before diving deep underwater in pursuit of fish. On other days, tatters of gray mist float across the landscape—sliding up deep ravines where deer and elk browse daintily, and hovering above the cranberry bogs and the fields abloom with lilies and daffodils.

One August day in southern Oregon, on a bluff overlooking the vast Pacific, a young journalist and I looked out upon a world drained of color—its edges swallowed by fog. Mostly it was the sound of the surf, the screeching of gulls, and the tang of salt in the moist air that defined the setting.

"Look at it," he said, raising a hand in a wide arc from the wind-twisted branches of the coast pines nearby to the beach dimly discerned below. "The fog deepens the magic of the coast. It has an eerie monochrome beauty that takes hold of you. When I see fog and mist, I know it's where I belong."

Little so evokes the Northwest coast as a vista veiled by fog, but my journey in late summer from the Oregon-California border to Washington's Cape Flattery began under sunny, cloudless skies. Before me the long, narrow land reached away northward for 500 miles to the Strait of Juan de Fuca with a rim of mountains at its back—the Coast Range and, to the north, the Olympics.

Thinly populated, the coastal strip counts few towns with more than 10,000 residents—Coos Bay and Aberdeen for sure, Astoria and Hoquiam hovering around that figure. Most people earn their living logging and milling timber, or fishing for salmon, shrimp, crab, and tuna. Visitors have added millions of dollars and thousands of jobs to the economy—the beachcombers who come to collect agates and driftwood, the people who come to hunt and fish, and the tourists who come to admire the scenic beauty.

I visited briefly at Brookings, my first stop along U. S. 101, which winds its way along the length of the Oregon coast, offering panoramas of the glistening sea and the surf foaming on the beach. But it took little time to learn that Brookings was one of the fastest growing communities on the coast.

"Until recently, Californians were buying up houses just as fast as they came on the market," said Bud Sorvaag, a real estate broker who moved from the San Francisco area nine years ago. "The newcomers are mostly retirees, lured here by the tranquillity and small-town friendliness and by the good fishing and the mild climate." The drop in California property taxes and high interest rates have slowed the trend.

Known as Oregon's Banana Belt, the Brookings area stays warm enough to grow lemon trees and palms, because it is sheltered from the prevailing northwest winds by a rugged shoulder of land. The same buffer shields the mouth of the Chetco River, making the harbor one of the safest of the 11 coastal ports in Oregon and ideal for the angler who wants to take to the ocean to troll for salmon in his own small boat.

In partnership with the Pacific, the Coast Range and Olympic Mountains both endow and define this edge of the Northwest. The cool, moist ocean air, caught by the barrier of peaks and dispersed as rain and snow, nurtures dense forests, grassy valleys, and rushing rivers that in turn foster logging, dairy farming, and commercial and sport fishing. Population remains sparse; no large cities have sprouted on this strip. Yet in the 500 miles from Brookings, Oregon, to Cape Flattery, Washington, the spectacle of mountains meeting ocean in myriad forms draws millions annually to visit.

Another contingent of anglers congregates around Gold Beach, where the Rogue River spills turbulently into the sea. I could have driven the 27 twisting miles from Brookings in 40 minutes; instead it took several splendid hours. I stopped at scenic overlooks, walked along grassy headlands rising abruptly hundreds of feet above the sea, and hiked down to secluded beaches nestled between rocky capes and massive bluffs.

At Samuel H. Boardman State Park, one of 70 state parks that preserve much of Oregon's spectacular coast for public use, I stood at House Rock viewpoint and watched the waves crash with ceaseless fury against the jagged sea stacks rising darkly from the ocean floor. I could see wooded Cape Sebastian far to the north and a series of scalloped beaches and rugged bluffs to the south—a view little changed from the days when European mariners first coasted these wild shores in their wooden galleons.

Often credited as the first to come was a Portuguese pilot, Bartolomé Ferrelo, a member of a Spanish expedition from Mexico in 1542. Next came the Englishman Sir Francis Drake in the summer of 1579 in his famous *Golden Hind,* hoping to find a sea route back to the Atlantic. Eventually the search for the fabled Northwest Passage drew the English explorers James Cook and George Vancouver and the Bostonian Robert Gray to this coast in the late 18th century; when Cook's crew discovered that the Chinese would pay a fortune for sea otter pelts, the tide of civilization began to move in.

In time it brought Archie P. Boyd from Missouri to Gold Beach and the Rogue River, which he says is as near to heaven as he can ever expect to get. "The Rogue's got everything—rough water, good fishing, and scenery people write books about."

A guide on the Rogue for more than half

Deceptively alluring, Devils Churn sparkles in the sea's retreat, but at high tide the waves slam into the chasm, at times erupting into sixty-foot fountains. The surf's onslaught chiseled out a cave, then razed the roof, thus forming this cleft. The Pacific also pummels some caves into arches, eventually into sea stacks. At nearby Cape Perpetua, this magnificent clash during gales attracts off-season tourists just to storm watch.

a century, Archie remembers when "so many salmon returned up the river to spawn and die that the smell would knock you down. Now you seldom see any salmon along the banks."

Archie, a vigorous 83 with wisps of white hair framing his ruddy, cheerful face, joined me for a short drive on the road that follows the Rogue for some thirty miles. We passed scores of anglers lining the banks, standing thigh-deep in the sparkling water in long rubber boots.

"The good ones," Archie said "know which lures to use in fast water and which ones in slow, and they know where the fish will hold when they get tired. But mostly good fishermen are spawned like a salmon on a stump—it's in our blood."

Upstream the Rogue cuts deeper through the coastal mountains. It boils and tumbles through a canyon wilderness, where great blue herons stalk the shallows on long spindly legs; where ospreys build nests atop tall, dead

> **"In certain respects Hathaway Jones symbolizes the mavericks and romantics who can feel at home in the solitude of a Pacific beach, who find exhilaration in the fierce storms that batter the land, and who are undaunted by the gloom of leaden skies that can last for weeks."**

snags; where people are few and where deer, otter, beaver, and bear thrive; where mountain slopes are so steep that the thick stands of Douglas fir seem to grow in stacked tiers reaching to the sky.

This precipitous country was the homeland of Hathaway Jones, last of the mule-team mail carriers. He served the isolated few who eked out a living mining, fishing, and hunting in the Rogue River wilderness in the years from 1898 to 1937. Hathaway was also

one of the great storytellers of the Northwest—with a gift for stretching the truth. He could kill a bear so large it yielded 21 gallons of grease, and he took pride in firing a very slow bullet. When asked about a deer that had been shot seven times, he snarled, "Only shot 'em one time . . . right through the heart, but he run quite a ways 'fore he drapped. . . . he run so fast, dodging trees this away and that away, my bullet jest went in and out . . . a-makin' all them holes."

On one of the trails that edge sheer cliffs, Hathaway fell to his death, but his tall tales remain part of the lore of the Northwest. In certain respects Hathaway Jones symbolizes the mavericks and romantics who can feel at home in the solitude of a Pacific beach, who find exhilaration in the fierce storms that batter the land, and who are undaunted by the gloom of leaden skies that can last for weeks, bringing as much as eighty inches of rain along the ocean, more in the mountains.

In Coos Bay, one of the world's largest ports for shipping timber products, I met another rugged individualist—Gordon Ross, a gregarious dairy farmer with a broad smile and a warm handshake, who is one of the few people licensed to sell raw milk.

The cows had left the pasture and were back at the barn for milking when I arrived. Creatures of habit, they filed into the milking parlor in the same order that they did each day. Gordon talked above the soft chug of the milking machine and the occasional lowing of the cows. He noted that the relatively few milk farms left in the Coos Bay area were producing as much milk as the hundreds in operation in the 1940s. In past times, he recalled, "boats plied the inlets and sloughs carrying the milk to the creamery early in the morning. If we needed anything in town we'd phone our order, and it would be deposited on our wharf when the *(Continued on page 48)*

"I work ground to grocery," says Gordon Ross, pausing to chat after delivering his milk to a market near Coos Bay. Embodying the pioneer spirit of his ancestors on this coast, Ross works every step of the dairying process, from growing forage to distributing the end product—old-fashioned, unpasteurized

CHERRY GROVE WHOLE MILK 1.89 GALLON

milk. *Self-sufficiency, a family tradition of four generations, has developed into a personal mission. For Ross, the hope of the future lies in people knowing how to fend for themselves.*
FOLLOWING PAGES: *Serving small boats and oceangoing freighters alike, Heceta Head Light penetrates the natural camouflage of foul weather that stymied explorers for centuries. Mariners searching for the Northwest Passage overlooked or underrated these bountiful shores, so often veiled in fog, until fur-trading ventures established a colonial foothold in the early 1800s.*

COTTON COULSON

boat returned in the afternoon. Now we've traded that convenient system for autos, gas bills, insurance, and repair bills."

In the bright but blustery day that followed, I meandered among the towering dunes that extend for 51 miles along the central Oregon coast—a chain of wind-rippled, tawny hills of smooth, soft sand that reflect the light like snow. The dunes owe their existence to the easily erodible mountains to the east. Although most of the coastal mountains consist of tough volcanic rock, this segment is built primarily of softer sedimentary deposits, which the rivers are gradually washing into the sea. Ocean currents sweep these great quantities of sand back on the beach, where prevailing westerly winds carry the debris of mountains as far as $2\frac{1}{2}$ miles inland.

Trudging in the loose sand soon turned my excursion into a vigorous hike, while a heavy northwest wind assailed me with a steady barrage of stinging sand. Unusually constant and strong, the wind was also adding to the woes of salmon trollers along the Oregon coast. The rough seas were tearing up their fishing gear, and the winds, by scattering the schools of herring, were dispersing the salmon that swarm on them to feed.

From Brookings to Astoria, in waterfront coffee shops along the length of the Oregon coast, I heard salmon trollers tell the same story of hard times in voices tight with anger and frustration.

In Newport I joined a group sipping bottomless cups of coffee in a fisherman's cafe. No one disputed the need to halt the decline in salmon numbers, but trollers were sounding off against regulations that had cut the prime time off their traditional season for the coho—the coast fisherman's bread-and-butter species of salmon.

Others complained bitterly that the state hatcheries were selling millions of eggs to the corporate fish farms. Everywhere I went the fishermen feared that these multimillion-dollar operations would eventually be in a position to control the salmon industry. The state hatcheries, I was told again and again, should be raising fish to rehabilitate the coho runs in Oregon streams that have been damaged by pollution and siltation.

Although hatcheries can protect salmon in their early stages of life, when predators, flooding, drought, disease, and temperature changes normally take a heavy toll, these facilities may encounter additional problems. Take the herons' nightly raids at the Big Creek State Hatchery near Astoria.

"The herons fly in at dusk. Then when the staff is gone, the birds go up on the walkways and flap their wings to get the water boiling a bit," manager Ray Sheldon told me. "We feed the fingerlings by throwing pellets of food to them, so when the herons agitate the water, the fish think they are going to be fed, and they swim over. Then the birds just help themselves." The hatchery crew countered with noisemaking cannon that go off through the night. And it seems to work.

Biologists such as Harry Wagner, of the Oregon Department of Fish and Wildlife, believe that hatcheries are not the panacea people once thought they were.

In recent years, said Harry, large releases of hatchery-raised fish have not translated into more adult salmon. They don't survive in the ocean as well as wild fish.

"In the wild," Harry continued, "the salmon populations have adapted to their home streams, resulting in genetic differences we sometimes don't fully understand or even recognize. Take the stock we released into the Nehalem River a few years ago. It had no resistance to a parasite in those waters and so was soon wiped out."

Hatcheries cannot replace wild fish, he

asserted. For that reason harvest quotas are based, in part, on the numbers of wild coho salmon returning to spawn in unpropagated streams—those where no hatchery fish have been released. "It's the only way we have to preserve the wild stock, and unless we succeed the long-term productivity of salmon may be jeopardized," he concluded.

"That means you can have a million fish out here, but we're being regulated on the basis of what goes up on unpropagated streams," said Herb Goblirsch, aboard the *EZC* as he steered carefully past the other trollers still lying at anchor, their outrigger poles bristling like giant antennae.

After a two-hour run, Herb throttled down to trolling speed, less than three knots. A gurdy—a large spool—slowly unreeled one of the three steel trolling wires hanging from one outrigger pole, and Irene Slevin, Herb's pixie-faced crew, snapped on short lengths of line with hooks baited with herring at intervals of 24 feet. Herb at the same time baited

" 'Why do I keep fishing?' Herb echoed my question. 'Well, there are those times when everything goes right and every hook is full. Then there's nothing like it in the world! 'Maybe, just maybe, tomorrow will be that kind of day.' "

the lines on the other pole. When all six trolling wires were out, each one weighted with a 40-pound lead "cannonball," $1,056 worth of gear and bait had slid into the sea. Now there was little to do but wait and watch for the tips of the poles to jiggle.

Through the sparkling day the boat rolled across the dark heaving surface of the open sea, until the sun slipped below the long horizon. In the boat's hold, chilled by a ton of ice, lay two dozen silvery salmon—a catch

little better than breaking even for the day.

"Why do I keep fishing?" Herb echoed my question. "Well, there are those times when everything goes right and every hook is full. Then there's nothing like it in the world!

"Maybe, just maybe, tomorrow will be that kind of day."

A few miles north of Newport, I scrambled down a steep slope to where the ebbing tide had exposed seaweed-covered rocks and the tidal pools of Boiler Bay. Seaweed of many kinds billowed in the shallows—their tangle of fronds anchored to rocks by rootlike holdfasts at the base of each stalk. Slippery and wet, the emerald-green sea lettuce, the broad brown blades of rubbery wrack, and the yellow-brown rockweed with small air bladders that popped when I stepped on them formed a richly textured tapestry.

The intertidal zone, sheltered by these algae from the full impact of the waves, teems with life. A cubic foot may have as many as 5,000 animals of 20 or more species. Crabs, starfish, sea urchins that look like purple pincushions, and sea anemones with flowery tentacles can stay submerged in the tidal pools, which rarely dry up. Higher on the beach, barnacles and purple-shelled mussels seal themselves to the rocks with their own cement and await the returning tide to filter plankton from the sea.

As far north as the towns of Cannon Beach and Seaside, a highway hugs the coast much of the time. However, near Lincoln City, a touristy strip of motels, U. S. 101 jogs inland through the rich dairy country that surrounds the town of Tillamook, famed for the full flavor of its cheddar cheese.

People there still talk of the Tillamook Burn of 1933, one of the most devastating forest fires in history. The fire raged in a 15-mile wall of flames, burning with a roar that sounded like the pounding of a dozen surfs.

"The playful wind, not angry, tearing or cold . . . but mischievous" takes shape
as a clay mask in the hands of Keiko Nakadate. Capturing in art forms the natural
forces around her on Oregon's northern coast, Keiko molds the changing moods
of surf, wind, and rain into murals, masks, and freestanding sculptures.

Snags 150 to 200 feet high blazed like enormous torches. Ash rained on ships 500 miles at sea and coated the streets of towns along the coast. It consumed almost 12 billion board feet of prime timber—enough to build a million five-bedroom houses—and left an area of some 375 square miles a wasteland of blackened stumps and trees.

Since then, three more fires have broken out, but now the Tillamook Burn has turned

"Great stands of virgin timber . . . once dominated not only the landscape but also the economy. They brought fortunes to a few and a unique way of life to the burly, hard-drinking, brawling logging crews who cut away so much of the primeval wilderness."

green again after one of the largest forest rehabilitation projects ever attempted, with sowing by helicopter as well as by hand.

Trees tell another story in Washington's land between the Olympic Mountains and the sea, setting a theme of beauty, riches, and controversy, in the wettest region in the continental United States. Great stands of virgin timber—Sitka spruce, Douglas fir, hemlock, and western red cedar, mammoth in size and astounding in their majesty—once dominated not only the landscape but also the economy. They brought fortunes to a few and a unique way of life to the burly, hard-drinking, brawling logging crews who cut away so much of the primeval wilderness.

I had crossed the great Columbia River on the four-mile-long bridge into Washington, and was on my way to the port of Grays Harbor. The surrounding hills had been the heart of the coast's timber-rush country at the turn of the century, when the forests rang with the sound of steel and the sawmill towns were scenes of carousing and revelry.

Today loggers no longer live in camps for six months at a time, sleeping in bunks on straw called "California feathers." The crews no longer eat together in a mess hall, where they might, as one local historian records, "indicate their displeasure with the food by heaving it out of the window without bothering to raise the sash." Loggers, however, still excel in the use of profanity; their mouths still bulge with "snoose," the snuff they use in place of cigarettes, which are a fire hazard in the woods. They are still a generous bunch, and if a logger gets in trouble, he can count on help. And the port of Grays Harbor is still one of the world's largest shippers of timber loaded as logs.

Unprocessed logs, I learned, account for 60 percent of the value of Washington's wood-product exports. Many feel exporting so many logs and so little lumber is destroying smaller mills and depriving the United States of timber it will need for itself.

But the problem is predictably more complex. Earnings from state-owned timberlands support school construction, so the Washington Department of Natural Resources is under pressure to earn as much revenue as possible. And the Japanese generally offer higher prices than domestic mills.

North of Grays Harbor and the sawmill towns of Aberdeen and Hoquiam, the land was once the domain of the Quinault, the Quileute, and the Makah Indians, who hunted whales and seals and raided and traded in large oceangoing canoes. To this day, Indians outnumber whites along much of the shoreline between Grays Harbor and the town of Neah Bay on the Strait of Juan de Fuca; but most of the land is government owned, and the Indians live on reservations.

Guy McMinds, director of the Quinault Department of Natural Resources and Development, a tall, sturdy man with strong arms

Tides of tourist traffic roll into the resort of Seaside—summer tides creating a landscape far different from any seaside wrought by the ocean. The first recorded visitors—members of the Lewis and Clark expedition who came over from nearby Fort Clatsop in 1806 to boil water for salt—left memoirs describing only "open waving prairies of sand" at the shore.

and the typically short legs of the canoe Indians, was waiting for me in Taholah, a sprawling community of 950.

"In the old days the sea, streams, and forests brought us an abundance of food, and life was good," Guy told me as we headed north of town. "There was time for leisure and riches for our great potlatches. Guests at these feasts could number in the hundreds, and hosts would give a lifetime of savings away for the sake of honor and prestige. Now these potlatches are a thing of the past. Our skills in basketry and woodcarving barely survive. Only the elders speak the old language.

But our respect for nature remains the same."

We came to a halt before a scene of awesome desolation. Gigantic stumps, broken trees, and masses of branches smothered the land beneath a monstrous welter of litter.

"Thousands of ravaged acres have been lying fallow and unproductive under burdens of slash like this," said Guy, barely containing his anger. This resulted, he insisted, from the past years of mismanagement by the Bureau of Indian Affairs. Logging companies had been permitted to operate on a cut-and-run basis. In recent years, he acknowledged, management practices have improved.

In the national forests, the United States Forest Service often requires loggers to concentrate much of the debris within the cutting tract. Crews then come in with prescribed burning to reduce the residue and prepare the land for reforestation.

Whether the land is public, or private, or Indian, man has cut down the mighty trees that ranked among the tallest in the world. Except for the stands in Olympic National Park and the cherished giants in other state and federal preserves, most of the old-growth forests along the coast will soon be gone.

The remarkably durable western red cedar, used for shingles and shakes, is already in such short supply that red cedar poaching has become a problem in both Olympic National Park and Olympic National Forest. At times it has also become profitable to salvage leftover logs, using helicopters to transport much of what was left on the ground in forests logged years ago. Where new growth has erased old roads, the pilot hovers inches from the treetops as he drops a cable through a narrow opening in the forest canopy to the "shake rats" cutting the red cedar down below. They tie a load of timber to the cable and the helicopter hauls the dangling cargo to a waiting truck.

As interest rates soared, however, crippling the housing industry and slashing the demand for timber, cedar salvage operations slowed, and countless logging and lumber firms on the Olympic Peninsula and throughout the Northwest also cut back or closed up.

"The shutdowns created a lot of unemployment, and hundreds were forced to leave the area," said Carrol Lunsford, a banker in the logging town of Forks.

In Clallam Bay, a tiny logging community on the Strait of Juan de Fuca, Crown Zellerbach announced that it was shutting down its logging operations for another reason—the corporation's Clallam Managed Forest no longer has enough trees suitable for large-scale harvesting by company crews. Though Crown Zellerbach has replanted its 82,644-acre site, the second-growth stands are years away from commercial size.

For many people in the area, timber scarcities threaten more hard times—and may eventually threaten Olympic National Park. In places like Forks, the views of sawmill manager Gerry Lane would find support. "The park is locking up prime forest land. It makes no sense," he says, "to leave valuable timber rotting on the ground or to let overripe trees stand until they are toppled by wind or disease. The park as it exists today is a luxury we can no longer afford!"

A downpour blurred the landscape on my trip to the rain forest in the Hoh River Valley—a dense evergreen jungle preserved in the park. By the time I arrived at the trail and laced up my hiking boots, slivers of sunlight were piercing the canopy of mammoth trees. Great fringes of moss hanging from the maples caught the light and glowed an incandescent green. There was no sky, only massive interlocking boughs with layer upon layer of needles or leaves shiny in their wetness. On the ground a variety of ferns flourished in a riot of profusion, cushioned by mosses, lichens, and grasses.

There in the park, in a fragment of wilderness, nature survives on a staggering scale that defies measurement in board feet. The rain forest's spellbinding beauty makes the words of Murray Morgan in his book *The Last Wilderness* profoundly apt:

"As long as the great trees remain in the park there will be men willing to cut them down, saw them up, and ship them away. . . . And there will be others—I suspect a majority—who would rather come to see them than have them sent."

Houses at Salishan, built to blend with the muted hues of driftwood, grasses, and sand, look out over a historic battleground of preservation—Oregon's treasured seashore. Growth in the 1960s of shoreline resorts and second-home communities, such as Salishan, prompted Oregon to clarify the boundary between public and private domain. In the battle that ensued, the state wrote into law its unusual and long-standing tradition of public use of the strand; the 1967 "Beach Bill" spotlighted Oregon as an environmental pacesetter. Today the public may wander more than two-thirds of the 362-mile shoreline, take in the view from 64 miles of headlands. Exercising their rights, scores of sportsmen at Seaside comb the beach for razor clams; biggest crowds turn out at "minus"—lowest—tides. Alerted by dimples in the sand, a clammer quick with a shovel can beat the clam at digging and net the mollusk for a chowder.

Spectacular stretches of the Northwest's sandy beaches inspire dreams daily, but never do fantasies come to fruition so fast—and then disappear—as at Cannon Beach during the annual Sand Castle Contest. Using spades, putty knives (left), air blowers, and even feather dusters, teams of seven people to a square have four hours to fashion their Camelots. One winner (below) evokes a far from idyllic realm, yet exemplifies a liberal judging policy on castles. Building castles in the sand here began as catharsis. The idea for a community contest arose in an effort to buoy spirits after the tidal wave from the great Alaska earthquake of 1964 wiped out businesses, the bridge into town—and consequently tourism in Cannon Beach. By the end of the 1970s the event had become so popular that the town had to set a quota on dream castles built on the beach. Tourism thrives again in Cannon Beach, cultivated with well-known attractions such as the contest, Haystack Rock (below, in background), and a major artists' colony.

Elephantine Sitka spruces and a lush backdrop denote rain forest along the Hoh River Trail on the Olympic Peninsula, wildest and wettest corner of the coast. Annual rainfall of 140 inches creates a superabundant world in the valleys. A black bear prowls forests, sampling fruit, fish, and the innumerable insects; an orb weaver spider waits amid the dew to trap insects. A tasty edible fungus called "chicken of the woods" grows on dead logs. High in the Olympics, snowfall usually ranges from 50 to 60 feet a year, and perennial glaciers lace the serrated peaks.
FOLLOWING PAGES: *At 6,000 feet and climbing, a mountaineer makes a September ascent on icy Snow Dome in the western Olympics, where rugged pinnacles look out on a rugged coast.*

Crimson-tinged huckleberries carpet Yellow Aster Butte a few miles south of the Canadian border. A lone hiker ascends one of several trails that web the glacier-carved slopes. Glaciers still carve Mount Shuksan, rising in the distance in North Cascades National Park.

The Cascades

By Cynthia Russ Ramsay

*I*n the high country of the mighty Cascades, with its steep, densely wooded slopes, its chain of snowcapped, smoldering volcanoes, and its hundreds of treacherous glaciers, danger is a fact of life.

Sudden storms can bring instant cold and driving snow even on what begins as a balmy July day. Winter blizzards and springtime thaws send tons of snow rumbling downhill with a terrifying force that snaps trees and tumbles boulders as big as houses. In summer forest fires are a constant menace as jagged lightning bolts rip across the sky, frequently striking tinder-dry trees and brush and touching off as many as 1,500 blazes. And from time to time, one of the still active volcanoes erupts with a staggering violence that spews death and destruction.

It was with the energy of more than 10 million tons of TNT that Mount St. Helens blew its top on May 18, 1980—blasting more than 800 billion pounds of pulverized rock and volcanic dust into the atmosphere. Sixty people were lost.

Other peaks in the Cascade Range of Oregon and Washington have claimed lives—since the turn of the century hundreds of backcountry travelers have become victims of death-trap crevasses, slippery ridges, or avalanches of snow, ice, or rock.

"The Cascades are tough country," said Ira Ford, a sturdy man of 88 whose face was remarkably unlined. In his time Ira logged, ran mail on a dogsled, and trapped lynx, marten, and fox all through the steep mountains that surround his summer home in the hamlet of Gooseprairie. "We have seven months of winter and five months of darn poor sledding," he told me. "And the snow is measured in feet—not inches. But there is no better place to live. It's so darn beautiful!"

The Cascades assert their beauty in countless ways—in the music of myriad waterfalls and the sweet silence of dense, moss-hung forests; in the pageant of clouds moving across the peaks and the sparkle of dew-kissed alpine flowers; in the gentle gaze of a black-tailed deer and the wild grandeur of the Picket Range, so sheer and formidable that only experienced technical climbers can venture into the area.

In addition to their wild beauty, the Cascades contain great riches in timber and in grazing lands for cattle and sheep. The swift rivers run with salmon and steelhead and other trout; and where dams impound their waters, hydroelectric projects generate power. Ski developments, resorts, and campgrounds make recreation second only to logging as money earners in the mountains.

From northern California the Cascades stretch north across Oregon and Washington, continuing into Canada where they are called the Coast Mountains. My journey crisscrossing the Washington and Oregon Cascades during the gentler days of summer began in the north—less than ten miles from the Canadian border as the bald eagle flies.

Still vivid in my memory is the trek to Copper lookout, 6,260 feet high in North Cascades National Park. An hour or so from the port city of Bellingham, I parked at the end of a dirt road and set out along a narrow trail to Hannegan Pass, for a rendezvous with Helen White, a backcountry ranger who patrols a wilderness of hemlock forests and subalpine meadows all summer long.

The trail led me ever higher above the roiling waters of Ruth Creek. A wren warbled an ebullient greeting; a grouse startled me with its low hoot; streams and waterfalls rushing across the trail splashed and gurgled their own soothing song.

Only these wilderness voices intruded upon my solitude as I hiked alone in the warm sunshine and clarion air. Finally, after I had

Born of volcanism, encompassing more than a dozen active volcanoes, the Cascade Range stretches 485 miles across Washington and Oregon. Lava and ash, left by eruptions over millions of years, account in part for the region's rich soils. Douglas firs predominate on the well-watered western slopes; ponderosa pines stud the drier east side. Volcanic cones— the Three Sisters, Hood, Rainier, the recently volatile St. Helens—rise abruptly above undulating hills. To the north of Rainier, the buckling and lifting of the earth's crust and glacial action have compounded the work of volcanoes to form a high, wild, and rugged terrain. Eleven national forests and three national parks straddle the range.

walked steadily upward for three hours, the forest gave way to meadow—still locked in snow. A trail of bootprints marked the way across Hannegan Pass, and then, with Helen—all smiles and surfeit of energy—I descended steep switchbacks to the wide gravel bars of the Chilliwack River. There I threw off my pack, devoured lunch, and discovered a little about the life of a backcountry ranger.

"At the beginning of the season we get 300 to 400 pounds helicoptered in—food and equipment; the rest we pack in ourselves," explained Helen, younger looking than her 30 years. "I see my job as an educator, informing the public not only of park regulations, but the reasons for them.

"In this subalpine region we do not allow fires—they can sterilize the soil, and the little deadwood available is needed by the environment to build up and enrich the soil. We don't allow random camping; plant life here is very fragile. We can also be helpful in an emergency—we're trained in first aid and carry radios."

For the next six hours, as we pushed across one snowy ridge after another, Helen amiably urged me on, promising the view would be worth the blister. Where the season's thaw had brought summer, fuchsia, monkey flowers, yellow wood violets, orange tiger lilies, and the diminutive pink blossoms of heather paraded their color in a landscape still mostly white in mid-July.

Long stretches of the trail remained buried in snow, and it was slow going uphill as I sank ankle-deep in the mush. On the descents I did better, glissading downhill with arms outstretched, bent slightly under the weight of my pack, with all the grace, I suppose, of a humpbacked dinosaur. In either direction I dreamed of dry, warm feet.

Still the view was a consolation, for by now the jagged, massive contours of Mount

Shuksan and the rounded volcanic cone of Mount Baker filled the southwest sky. To the southeast clustered the Northern and Southern Pickets, their lofty pinnacles of bare, gray rock somber and forbidding.

Finally we toiled up the last rise and came to our goal, a ridge surrounded by a spectacle of mountains in all directions as far as the eye could see.

By this time the world was at the edge of night. The sun was sinking behind the peaks, bathing the summits in a rosy alpenglow. To the east a full moon added to the magic, burnishing the snowy crests with silver. Then, long before we wearied of the sight, the mountains lost their shape, and there was only the snow, the black sky sequined with stars, and an ineffable tranquillity.

Perched on the ridge was a cabin with windows on four sides that gave a 360° view. Built in the 1930s as a fire lookout, it now serves as a one-room home during the summer for a backcountry ranger.

In recent years the government has come to rely less on such fire lookout posts and more on aerial reconnaissance, and when a fire breaks out in remote or inaccessible areas, planes drop parachuting smoke jumpers to combat the flames.

Smoke jumper headquarters for the region that extends from the Pacific Ocean to the Idaho border and south to around Yakima is located in the eastern foothills of the Cascades, near the small tourist town of Winthrop with its false-front Old West buildings, wooden sidewalks, and hitching posts. To visit the base, I headed east across the North Cascades Highway, driving slowly to soak up the scenery.

Near-vertical crags etched with snow thrust up from the dark forest and clawed the heavens. At first the swift-flowing Skagit ran beside the road, but then a series of dams harnessed the glacial river where it tumbled through a gorge, and created three mountain-rimmed lakes—Gorge, Diablo, and Ross—whose turquoise waters spin turbines to provide Seattle with electricity.

Crossing Washington Pass, I went from the wet west side of the Cascade Range, with its deep valleys and luxuriant forests of Douglas fir and western hemlock to the sunny, dry eastern slopes, where open stands of lodgepole and ponderosa pine and stretches of grassy meadows take over.

The Cascades themselves create the difference in climate and vegetation, for as the prevailing west winds sweep the humid ocean air inland, the mountain barrier forces the air upward, cooling it as it rises. Less able to hold moisture, the cooler air releases heavy snows and drenching rains. The winds have been wrung fairly dry by the time they reach the eastern side.

But not always. Lightning was crackling in the pewter sky when Bill Moody, manager

"By this time the world was at the edge of night. The sun was sinking behind the peaks, bathing the summits in a rosy alpenglow. To the east a full moon added to the magic, burnishing the snowy crests with silver."

of the North Cascades Smokejumper Base near Winthrop, launched into an explanation of his work. "Basically we're fire fighters, shoveling dirt to smother and cool flames, sawing down burning snags and trees, and scraping away vegetation to create firebreaks of bare, unburnable ground."

Later in the summer, when the danger of forest fire was at its highest, smoke jumpers at this base parachuted to 45 fires in a single week. In the wilderness lands to the north of

Stevens Pass these commandos fight 60 to 80 percent of the remote fires.

Though rugged and inhospitable, the North Cascades did not deter the ever hopeful prospectors who combed the mountains in the late 19th and early 20th centuries. They trudged up tortuous slopes, hacked out trails, and endured winters of terrible cold and snowbound isolation in their feverish quest for copper, silver, and gold. Rusted remains of their machinery, ramshackle cabins, mine shafts, and piles of tailings are scattered through the mountains.

Mining camps like Monte Cristo, Mazama, Silverton, and Gold Basin sprang up overnight and soon died as the grizzled miners abandoned their dreams. Most of the strikes promised more than they produced, and the rushes were short-lived because the ore was low grade and difficult to transport.

Like other mountain regions in the West, the Cascades were first explored by fur traders and trappers; the Scot Alexander Ross traversed the northern part of the range as early as 1814. Now neither furs nor minerals lure people to the Cascades; the green gold of the vast woodlands provides a bigger bonanza. Today tens of thousands seek to make their living from Cascade timber.

Take Kerry Dickson, whose calked boots, pants stagged—cut—to just above the ankles, striped twill work shirt known as a hickory, and hardhat immediately identify him as a logger. Watch him drive his 40-inch, 32-pound chain saw into a tree to bring it down precisely where he wants it to go, and you know he's an experienced faller.

The sweet clean scent of cut wood perfumed the damp air as I stepped warily across a snarl of fallen timber to meet Kerry at work high above the North Fork of the Stillaguamish River in the Mount Baker-Snoqualmie National Forest.

"We can't make the place a park and clear out every sapling before we fall a tree," said Kerry as he pondered a hemlock that soared into the heavy mist. "But we've got to avoid hitting stumps and other trees standing or already down; otherwise the timber will break up as it hits."

With his chain saw spitting wood chips, Kerry began by cutting a wedge-shaped piece out of one side of the hemlock. The precise shape and placement of this undercut would help determine the direction of the fall. Then he sliced into the other side, careful to leave the center of the trunk as a hinge. There was a brief moment of charged silence as the tree began to lean. Then the hinge snapped with a violent crunch, and the 150-foot hemlock thundered to the ground right where Kerry said it would.

But falling trees are not always predictable. Sometimes a tree is so rotten that the top breaks off from the vibrations of the chain saw. Sometimes a light breeze is enough to turn the tree as it starts to go over, for the canopy of branches funnels the air like a parachute. Sometimes loose limbs plummet down from above. Always there is a danger for the faller and the bucker, the logger who works beside him and saws the logs into 32-to-40-foot lengths to fit the mills.

It takes about eight weeks for two sets of fallers and buckers to cut a unit of 40 acres. Then the yarding crews come in. On the western slopes the crews rarely use bulldozers with grapples to haul the logs to waiting trucks because the land is too steep and the soil too easily erodible. Instead, a mobile rig with a tower and a cable system lifts the logs off the ground and hoists them in the air, up to the road.

I drove back down the long, unpaved logging road to the valley in the drizzle and slate-gray mist. The fog dissolved all

Refreshing cascade helps the Keep Kool Trail earn its name at Yellow Aster Butte. Though thousands of streams plunge down Cascades slopes, the range got its name from thundering rapids on the Columbia River that greeted early immigrants. Rangers suggest that visitors boil or treat the waters of Cascades streams to prevent intestinal ailments.
FOLLOWING PAGES: *Autumn fog fills the valley of the South Fork of the Nooksack River, near Mount Baker in the northern Cascades. Produce and dairy farms have replaced forests in this area, but timber remains the primary industry throughout the range.*

distances, so I couldn't see the lovely circle of mountains that surround Darrington. A logging and mill town like Packwood, Morton, and Trout Lake in southern Washington and Sweet Home and Oakridge in Oregon, Darrington differs in one important respect: Most of its 1,200 residents hail from the hollows and hills of North Carolina, and the people have kept alive the culture of southern Appalachia—quilting, raising their own peas, potatoes, and pigs, laughing a lot, and playing bluegrass and gospel music.

Grover Jones insists he doesn't play any instruments but beats on some—the bass fiddle and guitar.

"But Roy Morgan, here, plays a banjo, and he can make it walk a dog," said Grover in a soft accent that sounded out of place so far north and west. Grover was stretched out under a tree, supervising the painting of a ticket booth for the annual Bluegrass Festival in July, which attracts thousands. Neither Grover nor Roy nor the others in the three bands in town read any music.

"We just started pickin' a little. If the music is in you, you'll learn it."

As I traveled south, the topography beyond Snoqualmie Pass changed. From a labyrinth of glacier-covered mountains and a jumble of crags and barren summits and deep valleys that bewitched me with their beauty, I went to a mellower landscape, where stately conical volcanoes shimmered loftily above a sea of rolling green mountains. Mount Rainier, the tallest of the Cascade peaks, towers more than 8,000 feet above the surrounding mountains; like the other giant volcanoes, it was built up by a series of mighty eruptions of molten rock and ash that began less than a million years ago. The lower Cascades are also volcanic, but older than the major peaks, and were formed 5 to 40 million years ago.

There was no rift in the clouds to reveal Rainier's massive contours, so I decided to postpone my visit to Mount Rainier National Park and continued south. In the course of 50 miles I counted 10 black-tailed deer as I drove the gravel Randle-Lewis River Road, which took me through the 1.3-million-acre Gifford Pinchot National Forest, named after the pioneer American forester and conservationist. For Pinchot, the first chief of the U. S. Forest Service, conservation meant managing and developing the multiple uses of the forest for the greatest number of people.

Over the years grazing has declined in Gifford Pinchot National Forest. "Back in the 1920s and '30s more than 200,000 sheep filled these hills, but they're gone now," recalled 79-year-old Ernie Childs, whose shrewd blue eyes have seen many changes in the forest and the Forest Service since he started working there in 1921.

"Basque herders would graze their sheep in the high meadows around Mount Adams from June to October. It was a rough, lonely job trailing the flocks through the range, leading them to good feed and good water, watching out for stragglers and strays, and protecting them from bears and coyotes.

"These days, where are you going to find a person to camp out with a band of sheep all summer?" Ernie mused as we talked in Trout Lake, a small, serene settlement with a heart-stopping view of regal Mount Adams.

Ernie also remembers when the Mount Adams Ranger District had a permanent staff of two. "Now," he went on, "the Forest Service has a crew of 50, and almost all are involved in laying out timber sales and in reforestation." Of course, they also look after wildlife and recreation activities.

The biggest single change in the Gifford Pinchot and every other national forest in the Cascades has been the accelerated pace of logging. Until the *(Continued on page 78)*

In a town of transplanted Tar Heels, musicians compare their pickin' styles before a Sunday bluegrass session. Since the turn of the century, loggers have left depleted woodlands in North Carolina for the Cascades town of Darrington, Washington, bringing along their logging and music skills and their drawls. They—and their children, "second growth Tar Heels"—make up two-thirds of Darrington's population. Logging continues to provide a major source of income,

but residents supplement it in various ways. O. C. Helton builds log houses during slack times. In nearby Arlington, Mel Mortensen, a native of the area, digs potatoes in his garden.

Massive northeast face of Mount Rainier looms beyond hikers crossing a snow patch; 26 glaciers mantle the slopes of the 14,410-foot peak, highest in the Cascades. Formed from accumulated snows compressed into ice packs, the glaciers push rocks and debris that gouge and reshape the mountain as the ice slowly moves downward. "Strong men, brave hearts," a Yakima Indian in 1870 called the first two men known to have reached Rainier's summit. Today more than 3,000 attempt the climb each year. Frozen Lake, on Rainier's north side, emerges from the snowpack in the hot July sun. A ptarmigan hen in mottled summer plumage basks in the warmth; in winter she wears white. A profusion of buttercups, paintbrush, lupine, and fleabane brightens the fleeting summer in the high Cascade country.

Valley mist rises beyond Trillium Lake to garland the southern slopes of Mount Hood. Highest peak in Oregon, at 11,235 feet, Hood dominates the skyline to the east of Portland. Human presence— in pursuit of timber resources, or simply the magic of the mountain that includes

wilderness trails and a year-round ski resort—puts pressure on such easily accessible areas. Here the spotted owl thrives in old-growth coniferous forests. This night hunter, not often seen, preys on flying squirrels, rats, voles, and hares; it nests in the cavities of decaying trees. As logging expands, the owl population declines. Wildlife biologists study such species to determine the health of an ecological community. Researchers hope such studies will lead to programs that preserve sufficient habitat for threatened species—and thus ensure their survival.

77

Powdered in autumn snow, Mount Hood glows in the rays of a setting sun. A "glorious manifestation of divine power," naturalist John Muir wrote of Hood. Some 5,000 climb its summit each year; among the world's snow peaks, only Japan's sacred Fujiyama counts more. Yet even veterans find a challenge on Hood; five died in a single accident in 1981.

1950s logging was pretty much limited to selective cuts at the forest edge—taking the big trees and leaving the little ones to grow for future harvest. Now the forests are patched with clear-cuts, and new roads are shrinking the wild lands and shattering the isolation that had shielded the forests for so long from the onslaught of house trailers, motor homes, and the chain saw. Only 655 miles of roads traversed the Gifford Pinchot in 1949. Today the mileage totals more than 4,500.

The late Supreme Court Justice William O. Douglas, who hiked most of the Mount Adams country—"fished its high lakes," ate its "lush blueberries . . . and listened to the music of its conifers"—mourned the building of a road through forest there in his book *My Wilderness:* "Part of the charm of Bird Creek Meadows had been their remoteness and the struggle to reach them. Their romantic nature had been diluted. The mountain was still as magnificent as ever; the sky as blue; the fireweed as brilliant. But the meadows were no longer a sanctuary. They had become merely another spot on a busy highway, where the quiet was broken by the roar of motors and the sound of spinning tires."

Neither roads nor loggers may penetrate the Mount Adams Wilderness or the Goat Rocks Wilderness of the Gifford Pinchot. Since the passage of the Wilderness Act in 1964, ten such parcels of virgin forest, untrammeled meadows, and summits of ice and rock in the national forests of the Washington and Oregon Cascades have been protected by law, and a chorus of advocates is calling for the establishment of several more.

South of the mighty Columbia and its awesome gorge through the Cascades, the Oregon Wilderness Coalition campaigns to place the last roadless, undeveloped areas on federal lands into the wilderness system. On my way south to meet the leaders of the group, I made two stops—both resorts but dramatically different. Mount Hood, which rises to a height of 11,235 feet, seemed not quite real. Seen from a distance, it had an ethereal look—too ethereal for the jagged outcrops of volcanic rock and sheer ice walls, glinting malevolently in the sun, that loomed above me when I arrived at Timberline, America's first year-round ski area. A paved winding road had led me to the baronial Timberline Lodge, 6,000 feet up the south face, an island of luxury in the lap of the mountain.

I had planned only to sip white wine beside the monumental fireplace, but the perpetual snowfields, so accessible, beckoned. Next morning found me with rented skis riding up on a chair lift in the warm July sunshine. Soon all else was forgotten but the exhilaration of skiing. By 11 the snow had softened; a wispy cloud wreathed the summit. It was time to leave, for summer skiing ends at midday. Down below, when I turned southeast onto Route 26, I looked back and found that the summit had disappeared. Thick clouds had completely consumed all that dazzling brightness.

Sunshine is a more dependable commodity at the lavish Kah-Nee-Ta Resort owned by the 2,400 Wasco, Paiute, and Warm Springs Indians of the Warm Springs reservation. The resort sprawls across the hilly, rust-red plains just east of the Cascades, offering a multimillion-dollar lodge, golf, tennis, a stable of fine horses, and sunshine almost every day of the year. To end the day that began in snow, I lolled in the warm waters of a huge pool fed by mineral hot springs and watched evening shadows silhouette the sagebrush and juniper scattered across the rugged terrain.

I spent the next day in another kind of country—a lush, verdant realm where immense evergreens cloistered the trail, maples

Spires of Black Buttes jut near the western flank of Mount Baker, northernmost of the active volcanoes in the Washington Cascades. Called "white steep mountain" by Nooksack Indians, Baker averages 80 feet of snow a year; skiing lasts until the onset of summer. Scientists have kept a seismic watch here since 1975, when Baker vented vapor and ash.

and alders elbowed for space, and tangles of vegetation mantled the ground.

Members of the Oregon Wilderness Coalition were leading me through the Middle Santiam River country, an uncut island of old-growth trees in the Willamette National Forest—the most productive national forest in the United States in timber output.

"Now the timber industry, the most powerful single interest in Oregon, is exerting tremendous pressure on the Forest Service to log the Middle Santiam," said James Monteith, an articulate, energetic man in his thirties who is executive director of the coalition. "Conservationists contend that since nearly all of Oregon's productive forest lands have already been devoted to timber production, we should preserve this small remnant of the once magnificent old-growth Douglas fir forests of Oregon.

"If we were managing our existing timberlands properly, we wouldn't have to consider

> **"Even though lumber companies and the Forest Service now conscientiously try to replant clear-cuts, they are creating tree farms, and not forests. In a forest, trees are not all the same size and species. Tree farms have no thickets, no brush, no snags."**
> ANDY KERR, OREGON WILDERNESS COALITION

destroying our last wild forests. More woodlands in Oregon have already been cut over and have not regenerated than could ever be protected as wilderness."

Conversation ceased as we searched for footholds and fought for balance crossing a steep hillside slump, which had been triggered by the construction of a road. Great cracks in the earth and jackstrawed trees gave us some challenging moments.

"The instability of the soil provides another argument against logging here," said James, "for without roots to bind the soil and soak up the moisture, this kind of land just slides downhill." Forest Service soil scientists, I would later learn, do not regard the area as unsuitable for logging—though they agree that some parts are highly unstable.

"We need to have places like this," said Andy Kerr, associate director of the coalition, "because we're rapidly losing diversity, which is what keeps a forest healthy. Even though lumber companies and the Forest Service now conscientiously try to replant clearcuts, they are creating tree farms and not forests. In a forest, trees are not all the same size and species. Tree farms have no thickets, no brush, no snags, and no downed moldering logs, which provide habitats for a great variety of birds, insects, and burrowing animals. When the market is high, there's a timber shortage; when the market is down, there's a surplus. The industry has so overcut its lands here that job losses are inevitable. If anybody loses a job because of preservation, he'll simply be out of work a few months sooner. Let's bite the bullet now while we still have places like the Middle Santiam, and begin diversifying the state's economy."

Reluctantly I left my companions of the Middle Santiam. Along with their earnest arguments, other memories linger: rhododendrons blooming in gaudy pink clusters, the drumming of a pileated woodpecker reverberating through the forest, a dainty water ouzel diving underwater, our picnic at Donaca Lake, and the rich aroma of the moist, warm, fecund earth.

The following day I explored the Mount Jefferson Wilderness in Deschutes National Forest on horseback with Gilbert Ticoulat, a genial outfitter and cattleman with a weathered face beneath his Stetson. Tic, as everyone calls him, thinks this is not the time to keep adding to the wilderness system.

Right now, Tic claimed, we're only utilizing 25 percent of those lands because the Forest Service is not building new trails. As a result, he added, the public has access only to areas where trails already exist.

For Tic, a fast-walking quarter horse is the best way to see the country. And there was much to see as the trail climbed through the green, shadowed forest: little lakes bordered by hemlocks, shining like sapphires in the sun; light filtering through lacy gray-green lichens that festooned the trees; mosses, mushrooms, and lichens springing from deadwood downed by wind or disease; and puffy white clouds racing past the snowy summit of Mount Jefferson.

Tic reined up to let the winded horses "have a blow." Nearby stood gaunt, scraggly firs—the work of tussock moths, said Tic, adding, "If we don't spray, we'll be fighting them suckers with rocks and sticks." But the Forest Service sees no problem, and tends to let wilderness infestations run their course.

Tic wishes the Forest Service would let some of the natural forest fires take their course. "Those lightning strikes would burn up all this slash that is suffocating the forest floor. The logs, limbs, and pine needles lie like a tarp on the ground, and hardly anything grows underneath." We paused again before a lava field, a black and brooding lunarscape with a demonic beauty of its own.

Farther south—more than a hundred miles away—another cataclysm of the earth created a sight more breathtaking to behold. Some 7,000 years ago a volcanic eruption, 42 times more powerful than the explosion that rocked Mount St. Helens in 1980, left an immense crater that has over the centuries filled with water unbelievably blue. Crater Lake, centerpiece of a national park and considered one of the natural wonders of the world, draws a steady stream of awed visitors. So does the noble giant of the Cascades, 14,410-foot Mount Rainier. A spell of clear weather sent me speeding back north to that immense creation of ice and volcanic rock, whose summit challenges thousands of climbers each summer.

The summer of 1981 was one of tragedy and triumph on the heights of Rainier. On a bright June morning an ice avalanche buried 11 climbers in the worst accident in U. S. mountaineering history.

"We were plodding upward through knee-deep snow, and the guides told us to take a break," recalled 40-year-old Larry St. Peter of Edmonds, Washington, who barely escaped. "The day was gorgeous and so was the view as we rested some 11,000 feet up on the east face. Suddenly it happened. There was a loud crack, and the whole mountain seemed to be coming down on us."

A huge wall of ice had sheared off and shattered into massive chunks. In seconds the ice avalanche had crashed down toward the party of 28, including 6 guides. The 11 victims were swept into a crevasse and buried beneath 80 feet of rubble.

Days after, Rainier was the scene of a great triumph—when 11 disabled men and women attempted the peak on July 3. Seven are blind; two are deaf; one is an epileptic; and one lost a leg in Vietnam. Nine made it to the top. All had, in the words of Jim Whittaker, their leader, "already climbed the highest mountain of their own humanity: They had triumphed over their disability."

Not only for these climbers but also for those who hike, fish, watch birds, or delight in flowers, the Cascades promise special joys. Though I said my farewells to these mountains from an alpine meadow shimmering with small, bright colors, I would have much preferred to keep going, up one slope and down another.

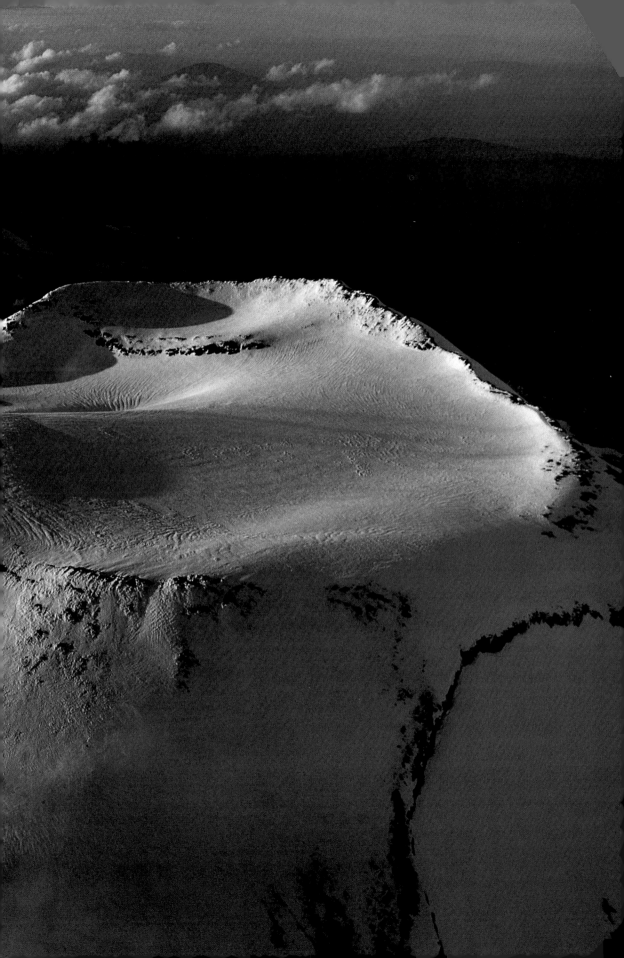

The Eruption of

Too vast for a single blink of the camera's eye, the ash cloud from Mount St. Helens spews 10 miles up and 50 miles across, filling a montage of 11 pictures. The roaring mountain appears here as a tiny slope at the right edge of the "mushroom" stem. Though the peak had been rumbling since March, it took the world by surprise at 8:32 on the morning of May 18, 1980, with a blast equal to 500 times the force of the Hiroshima bomb. Hot ash and debris sped at 200 miles an hour to demolish everything

Mount St. Helens

By Rowe Findley

within a 15-mile arc to the north. At his farm 31 miles away, Rocky Kolberg shot frame after frame—producing a montage, much more powerful than a single wide-angle photograph. Perspective distorts the height of the airliner flying by at 16,000 feet—lower than the cloud top. "The cloud took five minutes to reach its full height," said the amateur photographer. "There was no sound at all. How many things does a person see in his life to measure up to that?"

ROCKY KOLBERG, PHOTOGRAPHER; JAMES F. KOLBERG, DESIGNER.
TOLEDO POSTER CO.; TOLEDO, WASHINGTON.

ERUPTION

Before: Though wisps of steam vent a warning in April 1980, Mount St. Helens flaunts the beautiful face that had made it one of Washington's principal recreation areas. Indian myths personified the mountain as a fair maiden. Regarded as the most active of Cascades volcanoes, the peak had rarely remained quiet for more than a century during the past 700 years. It last erupted in 1857, "presenting a grand and sublime spectacle."

In a few terrible seconds Mount St. Helens changed my life when it blasted away its crown. I have been an inveterate volcano watcher ever since. And I have learned this about active volcanoes: Like living creatures, they are forever changing.

I was fortunate to be within safe watching distance in March 1980 when the Cascades volcano first coughed itself awake with minor splutterings—and again on May 18 when it convulsed away 1,300 feet of its stature and half a cubic mile of its volume, a paroxysm that left 60 people dead or missing and cut a destructive swath across 212 square miles of forests, lakes, and rivers.

As a writer, I have been able to file most stories away in memory once written, but not so Mount St. Helens. The memories of the eruption, and of friends lost in it, are too

strong. The articles I wrote for the NATIONAL GEOGRAPHIC continue to evoke letters from people interested in the volcano or in volcanology generally. And finally, the mountain is continually calling attention to itself with another conniption of steam or ash venting, or with a new spurt of lava-dome building— all these preceded or accompanied by localized earthquakes.

Except for sky-high eruptions, the building of lava domes is just about the most interesting thing that Mount St. Helens does.

A lava dome forms when molten rock, or magma, squeezes up through the volcano's plumbing to the surface, like toothpaste squeezed from a tube. Since June 1980 Mount St. Helens has formed three domes and blown two of them partially away.

By June 1981 the third of them measured

After: *Ghostly visage of destruction rises above skeletons of a once-towering forest along the shores of log-choked Spirit Lake. The north-slope blast leveled 212 square miles of timberland, snapping 150-foot trees, destroying and creating lakes, killing millions of animals. The fair maiden's summit had stood 9,677 feet above sea level; now "smoking mountain"—an Indian name for the peak—rose only 8,364 feet.*

nearly 450 feet high by 2,000 feet long. It still seemed dwarfed inside the mile-wide crater. One toe of the dome protruded over the rampart of the crater's low north side.

As slopes of the charcoal-gray jumble of a dome steepened, blocks bigger than trucks broke away from time to time and crashed to the crater floor. Internal pressures in the gas-pocked dome at times blasted cannonball-size rocks into arcing trajectories.

Such missiles added to the diversions for Geological Survey monitoring teams. Team members must also watch where they walk in the crater because the surface is marked by hot spots and broken by yellow, sulfur-encrusted fissures that constantly change. "A crack three feet wide today may be five feet tomorrow, or it may have closed," said Susan Russell-Robinson of the Survey. "In addition,

parts of the surface are lifting, other parts subsiding. It is never the same."

The valleys and lesser peaks below the volcano wait uneasily for the next whimsical sculpturing by the mountain's violent hand. Dwight Reber, helicopter pilot who flew NATIONAL GEOGRAPHIC crews over the devastated areas, was struck by the suddenness with which the landscape was reformed on May 18, 1980: "I became aware that the whole North Toutle Valley had been filled up—and that made the hills look lower. All the familiar landmarks were gone." The valley floor was raised as much as 650 feet.

The fill came mostly from the mightiest volcanic landslide ever recorded, which followed the collapse on May 18 of the fractured north side of Mount St. Helens. It was this that buried Harry R. Truman, the 84-year-old

ERUPTION

Spirit Lake lodge owner who refused to leave, and lifted the lake's surface by some 200 feet. It also dammed side valleys of the Toutle, creating several new lakes.

Army engineers worried about the new lakes, especially one in the valley of what had been Coldwater Creek. It was now Coldwater Lake, and it had the potential for eating a new outlet channel through the erodible fill material and unleashing a flood of catastrophic scale upon the lower Cowlitz River. The river runs through low-lying populated areas of Kelso and Longview, Washington. Consequently, the engineers directed the building of a 3,000-foot-long outlet channel for the new Coldwater Lake, about a fourth of it cut through solid rock.

Microbiologists were testing waters for bacteria. Among those found was *Legionella,* one strain of which causes legionnaire's disease, a potential killer if not properly diagnosed. The bacteria was growing in several lakes near the volcano, and health officials began a watch for any sign of the disease.

But nature's touch was not all to erode or destroy; healing had begun. Three months after the big eruption, fireweed, asters, and skunk cabbage sprouted on some heights. Little conifers, hidden under the snowpack that lay on the highest ridges, put on spurts of growth. Blackberry, lupine, avalanche lilies, and pearly everlasting revived. The U. S. Soil Conservation Service tried to hasten the process by the airborne sowing of 21,400 acres of grasses; the Weyerhaeuser Company, owner of half of the devastated land, planted 5,000 acres of trees within a year.

By the summer of 1981, greening had spread along streambanks, up many valleys, and across higher slopes. Nature's reseeding was aided by the gradual return of animal life to the devastated area. The May 1980 blast had given it the appearance of a biological

desert, killing—besides the vegetation—an estimated 1,500 elk, 5,000 black-tailed deer, 200 black bears, 15 mountain goats, as well as cougars, coyotes, bobcats, hares, and millions of birds and fish. A year later I heard a killdeer insistently calling its name; I heard the warbling of a mountain bluebird and looked in vain for the turquoise singer. Ravens and hawks circled overhead. I heard reports of beaver on the Green River, north of the Toutle. The air was thick with gnats and flies. If the insects are back, I thought, the insect eaters could not be far behind.

Because Mount St. Helens lies in the Gifford Pinchot National Forest, the U. S. Forest Service has found itself among the most earnest of volcano watchers. At first the problem was to protect its own crews and the general public from the mountain, in cooperation with sheriff's deputies, state emergency service personnel, and the Federal Aviation Administration. But after May 18's scything destruction, the problem became how to deal with the wounded land.

Months of study produced eight possible courses. The Forest Service adopted one that was basically a mix of the other seven. It would manage 174,000 acres; about half the land includes significant geological and biological features—a living laboratory on volcanology. The plan calls for timber salvage and replanting of some areas, and for recreation, something for everybody. Environmentalists had wanted more land set aside, and the state of Washington had wanted less.

Part of the damaging flood on May 18 came from glacial ice that was suddenly catapulted from the heights of the mountain into valleys below, where a rain of fiery ash caused swift melting. This duel between ice and fire underlines a salient truth about the Cascade Range of the Pacific Northwest, with its dozen major volcanic peaks: Glacial

Grim reminder of 60 people left dead or missing, the battered car of one victim sits swamped in ash. Photographer Reid Blackburn considered himself safe at nine miles from the volcano. He managed to expose a few frames before retreating from the blast to his car, where searchers found him dead of asphyxiation. The eruption occurred on a Sunday, sparing hundreds of loggers; the day off kept them out of the area of devastation.

masses into the millions of tons lie atop the banked fires of the sleeping giants.

The glaciers live on the heights as a joint product of latitude—the Cascades reach up to 51 degrees North—and elevation. Many Cascade mountains stand only knee-high to the major volcanoes, which rise to 14,410 feet, in the case of Mount Rainier. From California northward, glaciers armor all the volcanic peaks. The heat in the mountains causes cracks and ventings at times. It is not unusual to see a steam plume issuing from the snowy crown of Mount Hood. There is a lake high among the glaciers of Rainier that never freezes. Mount Baker in the late 1970s shook, cracked, and triggered minor mud slides of earth and melted ice. Clearly, several of the mountains are on a setting labeled "simmer."

From dim prehistory into modern days, Cascades volcanoes have been a rambunctious breed. Some 67 centuries ago Mount Mazama in what is now Oregon blew its top sky-high in a blast 42 times greater than Mount St. Helens' May 18 eruption. Mazama blew away its insides and undermined its crater walls; they later collapsed into a six-mile-wide caldera that filled with water and created Crater Lake.

St. Helens is not the only Cascades volcano to erupt in our own century. In 1914-17 Lassen Peak in northern California engaged in varied ventings of steam, roiling ash, fiery-red lava—and laterally nozzled blowdowns of timber not unlike those of Mount St. Helens.

Show-off of the Cascades chain in the 19th century, St. Helens erupted intermittently from 1831 to 1857. The period also saw brief activity from Hood and Rainier. If there is a lesson in the recent past for the Pacific Northwest, it is not to count on St. Helens going to sleep again soon. And even if it does, another volcano could be waking up.

Dome of lava looms above Geological
Survey scientists inside the crater (left).
A month after the eruption, the first
lava dome emerged within the caldron
(right); fissures veining more than 600
feet of the dome's surface reveal its
incandescent interior. Vapor rises from
the mile-wide crater (above) opened
when the May 18 eruption blew away
a seventh of the once-symmetrical
cone. Thus the mountain destroys itself,
and as the domes build up and break,
and more lava pushes up, the mountain
rebuilds itself. Unlike the slow work
of erosion, the volcanic forces here
reshape the landscape with speed and
awesome power, before our eyes.

ANCIL NANCE. OPPOSITE: NATIONAL GEOGRAPHIC PHOTOGRAPHER STEVE RAYMER

ERUPTION *After a year the meager stream of the North Fork of the Toutle River still struggles through a wasteland of avalanche-choked channels. Hours after the height of the*

eruption, groundwater and melted snow and ice propelled mudflows below here at 50 mph, damaging or destroying nearly 300 houses in the valley. The river's temperature rose to 91°F.

Spring cloudburst soaks a sagebrush plateau near the Bruneau River Canyon in southwestern Idaho. On the horizon, a swath of crested wheatgrass—an exotic from Russia, planted for cattle to graze—has replaced the sage, the native brush that dominates these thirsty highlands.

Desert Country

By Mark Miller

I did not understand it then. I was alone and on foot a mile high in the desert mountains west of Boise, beside a scrubby juniper tree. The sun was low, and the rich, slanting light boosted colors to a fabulous intensity. The air was clear; I could see a hundred miles of rolling lion-yellow hills whiskered with blue-gray sagebrush. A golden eagle spiraled on a thermal overhead.

There was no sound at all, not the bark of a coyote or a falcon's cry—the desert silence so total that cowboys call it a noise. Then the wind stirred: airy sighs and whispers in the juniper boughs, faint whistles in the sage. Because I had done what travelers seldom do during a desert transit, which is to stop and walk out into it, the desert spoke to me. Though I did not then know the language, I felt a strange, transcendent peace; the voice was the most soothing I have ever heard.

Desert. Few words connote less promise. "Writers tend to describe the desert in polysyllabic words," wrote E. R. Jackman, who with his ranching friend R. A. Long wrote *The Oregon Desert,* which is to Northwest desert ranching what *The Compleat Angler* is to fishing. "They say the desert is unchangeable, immutable, inscrutable, unnatural, indefinable, uninhabitable. These words are poor, as I see a desert. It is dry, hot, cold, gray, hard, vast, and fierce."

It is the northern reach of the great sweep of desert land between the western mountains, a lonely realm of sage and greasewood in a region better known for timber and rain. Lying mostly between 2,000 and 5,000 feet, it is sometimes called the high desert and covers most of eastern Oregon, as well as south central Washington and much of southern Idaho. Hot and dust-blown in summer, freezing in winter, it languishes in perennial drought. Wrote Jackman, "Let's call it raw."

The Weston brothers call it fun. Mike and Jim are mercury miners. Mike is 74, Jim 75. They dig cinnabar out of a mountainside above the Alvord Desert in Oregon. Jim was a watchmaker; Mike had been in construction. Sharing an unfulfilled penchant for invention and adventure, they reunited as partners.

Something about the elemental setting inspires their genius for contrivance. The entire place is jury-rigged. A network of pipes carries spring water to a steep orchard of apricot, apple, peach, cherry, and plum trees. Sprinklers water vegetables. Mike likes tomatoes, but the garden didn't get enough sun, so he built a reflector of aluminum foil. It rotates atop an axle salvaged from a nearby ghost fleet of old Weston vehicles. The tomatoes catch the sun all day.

Like many desert dwellers, the brothers live underground, in a Quonset hut shoved into a hillside excavation. Tunnels radiate from the main space. One passage is a Rube Goldberg workshop of gadgets and inventions in progress. Another starts out as a bathroom and ends as a cold-storage locker. "I sprayed the walls with insulation," said Jim, "hung up the guts of a freezer, wired in power, and it worked." For a time the brothers got electricity from a wind-powered generator. They're wired up to rural electric now.

They're also wired into other things. From somewhere high on the walls I heard a partridge. Then a meadowlark, then other birds, in stereo, from speakers connected to microphones set out in the desert. "I like to hear birds sing," Mike explained as he punched a button on his tape recorder. More birds. "That's for when they don't sing."

We said good-bye at dusk. Down in the ravine below the orchard, a creek rushed noisily, fed by the melting snow high up in the Steens Mountain backcountry. I recited desert definitions: "Forlorn desolation?"

"Nope," Jim said. "Dry, I'll grant you.

In the rain shadow of the Cascades the Northwest's high desert regions sweep eastward, rough terrain of lava field and butte, and fault-block mountain thrust up at fractures in the earth's crust. The Owyhee and the Snake cleave canyons; their waters feed the Columbia, flowing seaward through scrubland. Other streams, typical of the Great Basin's internal drainage, find no outlet to the sea; the nation's largest freshwater marsh forms at Malheur. The cowboy West rides high—at Pendleton's rodeo, in showplace spreads such as the Alvord and the Whitehorse, in the round of running livestock under the big desert sky.

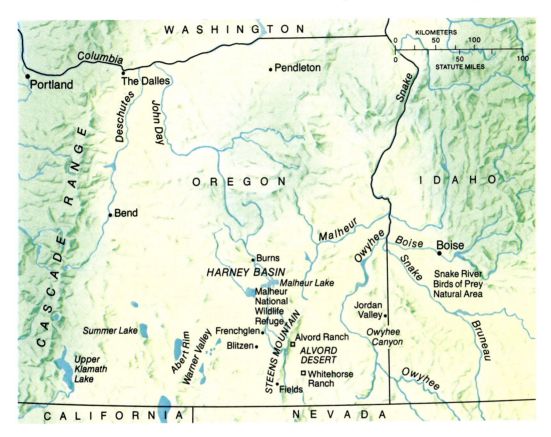

Uninteresting, no. Forget lonely. People drop in all the time to see what's going on. Friends, grandchildren, strangers." The air was cool and laced with the scent of lupine. The clay Alvord Desert playa turned pink, then mauve, as the sun set. Out on the flats a dust devil caught the last rosy light.

The Westons' digs look out on that desert, which is probably the hottest and driest region of the Northwest's arid country. "We get rainstorms now and then," said the manager of a nearby cattle ranch. "Had a ten-incher last month." "Ten inches?" I asked. "Between drops," he said.

In truth the high desert, cut off from moist Pacific winds by the Cascades, seldom receives more than 12 inches of precipitation a year. What moisture the region does get falls mainly on basaltic slopes of fault-block mountains. These ranges ramp warm winds up and cool them so rapidly that spring snowfalls and summer cloudbursts are common even as the dry beds of shallow saline lakes crack open a mile below. Winter blizzards can drop temperatures below zero—to a record low of –35°F. Let out to graze on open range, cattle and sheep roam as high as 9,000 feet in summer. In October they are rounded up and driven down to winter range below 5,000 feet. More often than by thirst, the stories say, the Northwest high desert has killed by freezing. *(Continued on page 103)*

Bucking the current, a teenager in Boise, Idaho, "surfs" on a board tied to a midtown bridge. Good for work as well as play, the Boise River provides irrigation for much of its valley.

High desert becomes choice property as suburbs sprawl onto the northern foothills of Boise. A spectacular view of Treasure Valley attracts an increasing number of the area's 114,000 residents to this higher terrain. Its porous soil, barely dampened by a 12-inch annual rainfall, requires constant dousing of lawns with city water. Idaho's capital, once a rest stop on the Oregon Trail, grows swiftly today amid expanding farmlands nourished by nearby streams.

Adapted to the desert, mercury miners Jim, at right, and Mike Weston share a Quonset hut wedged into a slope of Steens Mountain in southeastern Oregon. TV gives their underground home a window on the world. Sounds of the living desert enter through speakers—live, via outdoor mikes, or on tape. By transmitter, the brothers broadcast news of local weather. Each summer after mountain runoff subsides, they trek a mile to the mine shaft (far right) to chip away

at mud and rock in search of red cinnabar ore (right). Mercury trapped in the ore vaporizes at 600°F in a homemade furnace, then collects along the pipes of a condenser. The Westons aim for an annual yield of ten 76-pound flasks of mercury. Their mining chores done by late autumn, they go back to gadgetry—and enjoying the high desert beauty that lured them.

Rafters beach at Beam Camp, engulfed by rough-cut volcanic walls of middle Owyhee Canyon. The desert stream, runnable only in April and May, winds 300 miles through "the West's forgotten corner." Legend persists that the name derives from the homeland of hunters killed here in 1819. They came from Owyhee, today known as Hawaii.

In the main it is cattle country, its character, dialect, politics, and humor shaped by Old West attitudes, the endless labor of desert ranching, and the uncertainties of an increasingly marginal enterprise. In summer the walls of small-town stores are papered with rodeo posters. Top billing goes to Pendleton, Oregon, the Northwest's rodeo capital.

Nowhere more than in this dry country have people struggled on an absolute faith in the possibilities of land. Give an American his share of land, this faith holds, and he can do anything. I met few people who have lived here for a long time who do not cherish a personal version of this belief. Yet times are changing, and when the rest of America periodically declares testy, maverick Old West attitudes out-of-date, the people who share them retreat further into the traditions that have not failed them or their forebears for more than a century. Whether times are changing for better or not, I can't say.

"For years the desert was virtually ignored, except by the ranching industry," said biologist Caryn Talbot Throop as we toured the site of the new Oregon High Desert Museum near Bend, scheduled to open in 1982 with Caryn as curator. "Now we're looking to these lands for agriculture, coal, oil shales, uranium, geothermal energy, and recreation. Desert ecosystems are extremely delicate. We must learn to manage the high desert so it will serve us and still survive."

"Local interests—the cattle people mostly—get frustrated at our efforts to manage the desert lands they lease for grazing," said Steve Addington, a recreation planner for the Bureau of Land Management in Boise. I met Steve at a public meeting on a BLM proposal to study lands around part of the Owyhee River for possible wilderness designation. "Local interests mean people's livelihoods, important interests that should be given a lot of

weight. But this is public land, owned by all Americans, the majority of whom favor strict controls. Our objective is what we call 'multiple use'—for cattle grazing, agriculture, recreation, extraction of natural resources, and scientific study—plus appropriate protection of the desert itself."

"This land was overgrazed by 1890," said Denzel Ferguson, director of the Malheur

> *"For years the desert was virtually ignored, except by the ranching industry. Now we're looking to these lands for agriculture, coal, oil shales, uranium, geothermal energy, and recreation. Desert ecosystems are extremely delicate."*
> BIOLOGIST CARYN TALBOT THROOP

Field Station, a nature study center in the Harney Basin. "At Squaw Butte west of here some overgrazed plots have been closed for 45 years, and aren't even beginning to heal. The process may take up to 500 years."

Several days after visiting Denzel, I was on the Owyhee River's middle section in a raft run by veteran guide Jerry Hughes. Photographer Bob Madden was there, his raft piloted by Gil Hagan. In the supply raft was Gregg Leachman and his black Labrador. We had come to this canyon-locked stretch of the Owyhee in hope of finding the pristine desert we had been told no longer existed.

A bouncing 35-mile ride by truck led us to a put-in point at Three Forks, south of Jordan Valley. A herd of deer watched from the canyon slope as we shoved off onto the Owyhee, swollen, fast, and muddy from spring rains around its headwaters. Soon we were drifting through a thousand-foot gorge of volcanic rock and ash eroded into spires.

That evening we camped on a soft sand beach, beside junipers at the base of a towering basalt cliff. A common form of lava,

Canyon cameos: Fiery Indian paintbrush, an early bloomer, pushes up through the rocky soil along the Owyhee. The two-inch scorpion prefers to spend days underground, taking insect prey at night with pincers and curving poison stinger. East of the Owyhee, a stretch of canyon known as the Snake River Birds of Prey Natural Area, abounding

basalt underlies much of the Northwest desert, sometimes fractured into great fault blocks tilted up to form half-mile-high cliffs—such as Abert Rim in south central Oregon—or solidified into the fluid shapes of molten rock found at Diamond Craters in the Harney Basin. Where the lava flowed in thin, broad sheets and covered vast areas, the exposed sedimentary terrain around it eroded away, leaving stone-capped mesas.

Above our camp the canyon rims barred the entry of livestock from the grazing range that flanks the river, and clumps of native bluebunch wheatgrass stood knee high. Wild flowers exploded from every crevice. Partridges raced in chattering pairs across slides of broken rock. Swallows flew from mud nests attached to the vertical canyon walls. I slept to distant thunder.

Throughout the next three days we ran formidable rapids, stopping often to scout the safest passage. Along quiet stretches, Canada geese vaulted from riverside nests. Thrashing across the water as though crippled—luring us away from their young—they let us draw close before churning away once more. It is a beautiful, pathetic ruse.

Golden eagles soared high above the river. Otters swam on their backs, staring intently at us as we passed. A beaver paddled by, huffing through jaws clamped on a sapling. Tracks in the riverbank mud betrayed the presence of coyote, deer, and bobcat hidden in the brush. A more abundant natural place I have never seen. Professional guides like Jerry, Gil, and Gregg tend to express delight in such places by becoming very quiet. Resting their oars, they look around as if they had heard something.

"In the desert many otherwise sober people experience a feeling of profound serenity and spiritual rejuvenation," Steve Addington had told me. "I suspect it's related to the fact that man didn't evolve in the city. Instinctively, you know where you belong."

During the Depression of the 1930s many parts of the Northwest desert belonged to destitute people—cowboys down on their luck, out-of-work loggers, busted prospectors, and failed ranchers.

Inspired by the vastness of the land, invited by the Homestead acts, thousands pursued a dream of independence. Some made it, but many didn't. Everywhere, I saw their sad monuments. Near Ellensburg in Washington, a swaybacked hay barn, a house nearby, front door banging in the hot wind, windows as empty as the eyes of a skull. In the timbered northern fringes of the Oregon desert, a church, windows open to the rain, swallows nesting in the choir loft. In the Catlow Valley, the town of Blitzen nearly buried in dunes.

Many left the desert. Some managed to scrape by. More than a few built whiskey stills and produced white lightning. This has

"I wasn't prepared for this country.... People 25 miles apart called one another neighbors. It was hard to get used to the idea that I had to feed anybody who'd come by anytime of day, but those were friendly times."
GEORGIA CROW, A COWBOY'S WIFE

always been hardscrabble country, so, in spite of generally high standards of regional honesty, some lawbreaking seemed more respectable than the alternatives.

"I used to moonshine," said Johnny Crow, a desert native and longtime rancher whom I met in Burns. "I'm not ashamed to say it. We had to moonshine to keep off of the county." Johnny and Georgia, his wife of 44 years, live in a neat one-story house filled with the memorabilia of a cowboy's life. The day before my visit he had been out on the

in rodents and uplifting winds, supports one of earth's prime nesting sites for falcons, hawks, eagles, vultures, and owls.

range, on horseback, helping friends brand cattle. Johnny is 79. "I was raised on the desert," he told me. "Mother died of pneumonia when I was a yearling. Dad was a buckaroo boss for the Seven T outfit in Warner Valley. He ran 17 buckaroos and a cook. My older brother rode a mule, and on long rides I rode on the chuckwagon. We slept in a tent. Fun for a kid, rough on a man."

Georgia came West from Connecticut and taught school. The school district was broke and paid her with promissory notes. "I wasn't prepared for this country or the people," she remembered. "People 25 miles apart called one another neighbors. It was hard to get used to the idea that I had to feed anybody who'd come by anytime of day, but those were friendly times."

Johnny brought out studio photographs of old sidekicks, immaculately groomed, even a bit foppish in dark suits, starched collars, dimpled silk cravats, diamond stickpins, glossy boots, gold watch fobs, brushed-felt Stetsons and tweed newsboy caps.

"Those were genteel days," Georgia commented. "Cowboys then had a certain pride. Now a lot of it is make-believe, empty swagger. Being a cowboy isn't a matter of buying an outfit." Johnny listened carefully. "She makes my shirts, though," he said. "Beautiful ones." Georgia smiled. "Well," she said, "you're a real cowboy."

As more family ranches feel the pinch of soaring production costs and narrowing profit margins, the pressure to sell increases. The buyers are often investors, who rely on resident managers. There is no inherent villainy in this, but the trend toward absentee ownership worries locals who see themselves priced out of the land on which they were raised and dreamt of someday owning.

"This is agricultural land, not a big Monopoly board," said rancher Hank Vogler,

whom I managed to catch up with out on the range. He was tending sheep from horseback, a Winchester rifle in a saddle scabbard ready for the coyotes that prey on the herds. "What happens to the price of beef? To the people who know how to raise it, and are willing to? The American people lose."

Hank is 32 and holds a degree in ranch management, but when he rode up to my car, wearing a battered black hat, dusty overcoat, and worn leather chaps, his black-mustached face weathered by sun and wind and a chew of Copenhagen tobacco bulging under his lower lip, he looked as mean as any cowboy who ever rode across a movie screen. I felt it wise to explain that friends of his had urged me to seek him out. "That's okay," he murmured, spitting brown juice. "Nothing to do out here anyway except catch pneumonia and cuss the federal government." Another spit. "What do you want to know?"

Buffeted by a chill wind and sprinkled with rain, we talked a long time about the hardships and pleasures of Northwest ranching. The negatives are piling up fast, Hank said, whittling a piece of sage with his knife. "Answer me this: If you find your ranching earns you one percent of your land value versus 15 percent if you cash out and invest it, what're you going to do?"

Hank—Henry C. Vogler IV—is the third Henry Vogler to work the family's 35,000-acre Island Ranch. He and his wife, Cheryl, are raising four daughters and a son—Henry C. the Fifth. Whether young Henry and his sisters will have the chance to work the Island Ranch someday is by no means certain. "Sure you're sitting on a lot of land," said Hank, "but the actual in-the-pocket money most ranchers get up here would probably qualify them for food stamps. So why not sell out? I'll tell you why. Because you love this country and this way of life." *(Continued on page 111)*

Neck craned, a greater sandhill swoops low at Malheur National Wildlife Refuge on wings that may span 7¹/₂ feet. Nesting cranes, mated for life, stroll a marsh in this oasis, visited by more than a million birds each year—and thousands of birders. After nesting, some 3,000 sandhills gather at Malheur in autumn, gleaning grain before flying to California for the winter. Denzel Ferguson, head of a field study station at Malheur—though not part of the refuge—takes a strong stand against cattle grazing on publicly owned desert lands. Behind him appears a reason: Fencing divides a grazed field from one lush in habitat for wild tenants. Refuge officials maintain, however, that today's grazing programs generally aim at sustaining wildlife habitat.

National Wildlife Refuge

U.S. DEPARTMENT OF THE INTERIOR
FISH AND WILDLIFE SERVICE
BUREAU OF
SPORT FISHERIES AND WILDLIFE

UNAUTHORIZED ENTRY PROHIBITED

Expert lariat toss jerks a calf to a halt in the timed calf-roping contest at the famed Pendleton Round-Up in Oregon. Dismounting, the cowboy throws the straining calf by hand, then ties three legs together with the line held in his mouth. A century ago the cattle trade ruled Pendleton; riders honed skills at roundups to brand calves and claim stock. Today the town's economy centers on wheat, lumber, peas, woolens, and furniture. But when harvesttime ends, cowboy skills of the top rodeo professionals lure spectators in the tens of thousands to Pendleton's extravaganza.

Lodgepoles—cut from lodgepole pines—thrust from a cluster of tepees at the Pendleton Round-Up. Here Indians swap reservation life for camping and dancing in traditional style. Campers are paid—and pay heed to rules aimed at producing "a fine Indian show."

Merely to ride along as a spectator on roundups, I found, is exhausting. To wrestle with cattle, eat dust, and work under a desert sun knowing this year's beef prices aren't going to cover expenses can break your spirit. "You start thinking about that when you're pitching hay at your cattle on Thanksgiving Day and Christmas and any other urban holiday you can pick," said Hank Vogler.

There have been some changes. When Johnny Crow went into the mountains to round up wild horses, he rode in on a saddle bronc. "It injured horses and men," said Ron Harding, a specialist on wild horses with the Bureau of Land Management in Oregon. "In 1977 we began to use helicopters to start the horses onto trails and into blinds"—at a cost, I learned, of $75 per head as opposed to as much as $400 using men and horses.

Many thousands of wild horses—the exact number is disputed—fell prey to a growing demand for animal food, including canned pet food. Hundreds were selected by the Army for use or for sale to foreign armies. "Overpopulation may have led to starvation and die-offs, which is a natural corrective condition," Ron noted. "We estimate we have about 4,000 horses running wild in Oregon now. Nationwide, about 60,000."

Strictly speaking the horses are not wild but feral—the untamed descendants of once-domestic animals. Public interest in the horses, said Ron, led to the 1971 passage of a federal law "under which selected animals are assigned to qualified people for breaking. If they take proper care of them, we can grant a title of ownership. These are horses of superior intelligence which for many people represent the western heritage. We intend to protect and preserve them."

The protection of wildlife in the Northwest desert became a national issue during the administration of Theodore Roosevelt

when unrestricted hunting and the appetite of the millinery industry for feathers threatened to exterminate many species among the region's vast colonies of nesting and migratory birds. Public protest spurred Roosevelt to proclaim much of the Harney Basin marshland a sanctuary. Today the 183,000-acre Malheur National Wildlife Refuge shelters 270 bird species, including the dive-bombing peregrine falcon and the greater sandhill crane, a major nesting species here. Refuge manager Joseph P. Mazzoni, Bob Madden, and I rode to the northern end of Malheur Lake in a flat-bottomed boat pushed by an old Lycoming airplane engine and prop.

"Strange to find marshlands in a desert," Joe told us. "Internal drainage characterizes

*Seal of ownership sizzles into the flank
of a calf during spring roundup at the giant
Whitehorse Ranch in southeastern Oregon.
A horseman holding a taut line controls
the calf's movement as the propane-heated
branding iron does its work. Ranching knows
its gentler touches: A gnarled hand grasps a
shapely coffee cup, and a neat horse tail knot
reveals a ranch girl's pride of ownership.*

this region—our water doesn't flow to the sea—but our high evaporation rates can leave this lake bone dry in bad years."

Engine off, we drifted over a shallow part of the marsh thick with tall bulrushes, as a circling melee of great and snowy egrets upset by our presence descended to reclaim their nests. Wind in the bending rushes, the papyrus of the Bible, set up a resonant sound like thunder rumbling deep within the lake itself. We drifted past muskrat houses and bird nests of many sizes, constructed of rushes and floating on the marsh, most with eggs and a few with newly hatched chicks. The sky swarmed with birds honking, crying, whistling, screeching, and chittering, a fierce aerial protest despite Joe's careful approach.

"The colonies are mostly stable," he told us as we maneuvered past a nest. "But some, the black-crowned night herons for example, are troubled by loss of habitat and pesticide pollution elsewhere, problems we can't remedy from here."

Joe feels the sandhill crane population is in trouble. Most of the crane nesting habitat in this region lies on private land, more and more of which is being converted to farm use. The situation points to the importance of refuges such as Malheur. "Here we can try to maximize wildlife production," Joe said.

Limited grazing of livestock is permitted within refuge boundaries at certain times of year for habitat management purposes, but the strict controls placed on this land—some of the finest in the basin—rankles cattlemen in need of better forage. At the same time, the policy arouses the ire of environmentalists who favor total exclusion.

When I visited the college-supported nature study facility at Malheur Field Station, Denzel Ferguson voiced the strict environmental viewpoint that has made him less than popular among ranchers in the high desert.

"Running cattle on arid Western land," he asserted, "is no different from strip-mining in West Virginia. It employs people but isn't benefiting our society as a whole." As he saw the equation, Americans consume about 125 pounds of beef per capita per year, and only a couple of pounds come from this region. And most of that, he concluded, comes "from public land leased to ranchers for much less than the cost to taxpayers. I don't believe the return justifies the real cost in dollars and in terms of the environment."

I carried Denzel's objection out onto the range where rancher Hank Vogler, filling in for his two Basque sheepherders running errands in Burns, was camped in a teardrop trailer. "Granted at this point Western beef isn't very important," he said, "but as the standard of living rises around the world there's increasing competition for Midwestern grain we now feed to cattle. The Midwest farm we compete against now is going to grow grain for export because it'll be more lucrative. It takes a lot of tractor fuel to grow grain, whereas it takes very little to raise beef on range grass. Our time will come when Midwest production declines and demand for our beef increases, but it'll never be easy."

Among ranchers there is an old joke about why high desert horses are so fleet. To get enough to eat, it goes, the horses have to graze at 30 miles an hour. Behind the humor is a truth, which is that survival on the desert is never easy.

A single family of Northern Paiutes once required up to 100 square miles of desert for subsistence. When encroaching white settlement thwarted the Indians' nomadism, some joined the Bannock tribe in a hopeless resistance in 1878—ending with their exile along with other tribes to the Yakima reservation above the Columbia River in Washington. Granted land near Burns in 1934, the Paiutes returned to the desert, but not to the life they had known, or one for which they were prepared. They fell into abject poverty.

I talked with Jim St. Martin, the 35-year-old chairman of the tribe's General Council, in the modest new tribal headquarters. Sitting behind a paper-covered desk, his dark hair in a braid, Jim symbolized the meeting of cultures that lies at the heart of Native American problems. Lean, intense, and carefully articulate, he has the style of a Vietnam-era activist who has learned hard truths about the difficulty of effecting social change.

"Overt racism is for us pretty much a thing of the past," Jim explained, "but deeply ingrained stereotypes of Indian people persist, and they impede our efforts to enlist support for the tribe's economic development. Plus they hurt our people inside." Distinguished from most of his friends by his college education, Jim was studying for a master's degree in social work when the tribe invited him to run the government-supported job-training program. "I immediately saw the need for broader programs to put the reservation on its feet," he recalled. "Like agriculture and manufacturing. But that takes seed money. It's going to be a difficult road."

In these times a tribal leader's functions are less ceremonial and more bureaucratic. "I go to Washington to look for grants," Jim told me. "We're so small—240 enrolled right now—that I have to buttonhole them so they'll pay attention to us."

Plagued by substandard housing, the tribe has embarked on a construction program. "About 160 people live on the reservation," Jim said, "and the rest close by. Indian people choose to live together because they like a community life—the rumors, gossip, politics, and language. About 70 percent of the people under 30 can speak it. Here next to Burns, though, unlike tribes isolated by big

Tiny Frenchglen, rich in the aura of the Old West, welcomes visitors to the Oregon desert and the nearby Malheur wildlife refuge. Cattleman Pete French—the town bears his name—rode round these parts in baronial style until a homesteader shot him dead. At the eight-room hotel, a landmark in this town of 30, a flicker trying to drill a nest hole may provide guests with unsolicited wake-up service. The woodpecker earned the nickname "wake-up"—not for its tattooing, but for its ringing wicker calls.

reservations, we deal daily with downtown."

On the small reservation of some 770 acres, Jim noted, there are fewer resources and less authority to pursue traditional beliefs. "So you don't see long hair often," he said, "or beadwork or sweathouses. The differences are inside."

A key issue is the tribe's youngsters. "Indian kids tend to be shy and bunch together in public schools," Jim explained. "We've gotten Indian parents involved to improve instructional quality and help our kids achieve. But many are troubled, unsure who they are and what they want to be, and what the outside world expects of them. Sometimes downtown people don't understand that."

As I prepared to leave, Jim studied the spring afternoon sky. "I'm taking my wife and kids to the country when it dries a bit," he said. "I was outdoors a lot as a boy, in the high backcountry behind Mount Adams on the Yakima Indian Reservation and on the Columbia River. I used to watch the men dipnetting for salmon from platforms at Celilo Falls before the dam at The Dalles backed up the water over them. They'd smoke fish and live in lean-tos. It was an important influence on me. We try to take our kids to the country to camp and fish. The world's complex and difficult and we have to face it, but it helps if you go back now and then to natural places."

Natural places. All places were once natural, of course. Deserts stayed pristine longer than most other places simply because few people wished to live in them. When we did, we came mainly to exploit, and our industry obscured the sources of our inspiration. Secure enough now to stop and reconsider, we begin to hear what the desert—indeed all beleaguered wilderness—is saying to us.

Late one afternoon on the western reaches of the Northwest desert, I stood on

the reedy shore of Summer Lake. The air was cold, damp, and pure. The sky was crowded with weather—a snowfall to the north, moving across the plain like a sheer curtain. Due east, gray-blue thunderheads were underlit by the setting sun. To the south, dark clouds dumped rain and stabbed the desert with lightning bolts. Above, a brilliant blue sky and a vee of honking Canada geese. A rainbow domed above the lake, which shone like mercury. The far shore was a rich burnished gold. The panorama was incredible, like the paintings by Albert Bierstadt of impossibly beautiful landscapes. Yet here it was.

I felt the same exhilaration that came over me when I entered the desert a month before, 200 miles northeast of here. I felt as if everything had been wiped clean, and nothing we might do could surpass in perfection what I saw here. Then I understood what the desert had whispered to me before.

This is how it once was, it said. Here is a second, perhaps a last chance to use the knowledge and wisdom we've acquired to join culture with environment and nurture both at once. Doing the right things here, it said, offers a metaphor for reconciliation and balance everywhere. It said, yes, there is still infinite possibility in the land.

"The Alvord Desert . . . forming one of the largest and most perfect playas in the world, seems to burn lasting images upon the mind." So write Denzel and Nancy Ferguson of the 7-by-12-mile expanse of cracked, salt-crusted mud; spring runoff briefly turns it into a lake. Desert touring tops out at nearby Steens Mountain; a seasonal road—brutal to cars—runs to the 9,670-foot summit of this giant fault-block mountain. In its shadow the town of Andrews records Oregon's driest weather—about 7 inches of rain a year; temperatures have ranged from -33°F to 107. Yet Cactus Smyth, who has trailed cattle across Oregon, calls it home. His grandfather founded the town. "Like an old horse," says Smyth, "I always head back for my home range."

Sound of harvest breaks the silence in eastern Washington's Palouse Hills as a combine chews through wheat fields. Rich soils, heavy snows, timely June rains, warm summers— and farming ingenuity—create a grain-rich region across land once considered useless.

Farm Country

By Mark Miller

The gift of water—diverted from rivers and pumped from wells—greens valleys and plains of the Northwest's thirsty interior. Idaho "desert farmers" dig potatoes along the Snake; irrigated wheatlands line the Columbia's Big Bend. Apple blossoms brighten the Wenatchee Valley, and canals water the Yakima's hops and vegetables. More than 80 crops grow in the rich Willamette, where urban spread threatens farmland. Dry farming—without irrigation—wrests wheat from dusty Palouse lands south of Spokane, hub of the multistate farming, mining, and logging area called the Inland Empire.

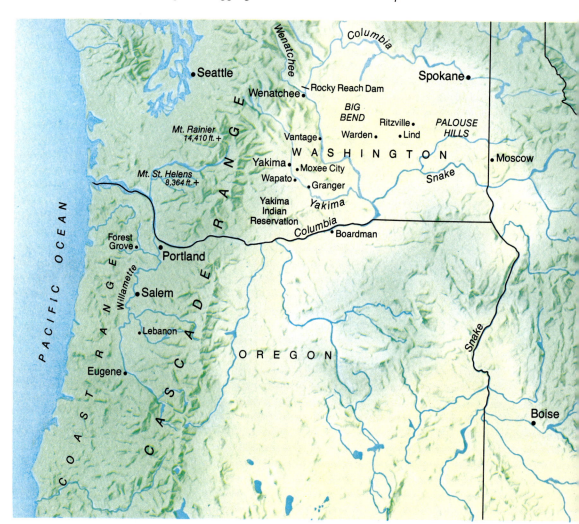

"There is nothing very glamorous about a bushel of wheat," a spokesman for Northwest shipping recently wrote, "unless you're hungry." I considered that as I stood on a windy hill in Washington's vast Palouse wheat region. A mile away, growling machines resembling enormous beetle-shaped robots gnawed through the wheat. Much of the world is hungry, and most of the Palouse crop, a major part of the Northwest's winter wheat harvest, would go to overseas buyers.

In one recent year Japan alone bought more than 80 million bushels of that harvest. Korea purchased 43 million. Bangladesh, its 90 million people languishing within a country not much bigger than New York State, ordered 21 million bushels. I held a handful of wheat and wondered how long it would be before it might pass as noodles between the lips of a Thai child, or stand as loaves of

KILOMETERS
0   50   100

0   50   100
STATUTE MILES

MONTANA

IDAHO

Idaho Falls
Shelley

Snake

the 1840s and 1850s pushed hard for the alluvial bottomlands of the Willamette River Valley in western Oregon, past the powdery flatlands of southeastern Idaho where today a quarter of the nation's potatoes and a third of its pea harvest are produced.

The wagon wheels broke through a crusty soil and raised plumes of stinging dust. The settlers could not have known it was rich in volcanic ash, 30 feet deep in places, or that it was far superior to many soils in the retention of moisture. Nor could they have imagined the vast underground water sources, the aquifers locked hundreds of feet under basaltic rock. Rain fell sparsely. Dry winds parched lips, and heat felled ox teams harnessed to the covered wagons. The emigrants pressed on and looked back with burning eyes on bleak treeless horizons that some day would soar in value, turning hardscrabble farmers into paper millionaires.

In the Northwest's regions of sparse rainfall, dry farming and desert reclamation through irrigation have brought much of the land into grain, potato, and seed crops. But the centers of its more diversified agriculture lie in the Willamette River Valley west of Oregon's Cascades, and in the Yakima River Valley of south central Washington, where a 2,000-mile canal system diverts river water to irrigate half a million acres, and 50 crops. In the Willamette Valley, government statisticians routinely account for more than 80 crops. North of the Yakima Valley, where the Wenatchee River meets the Columbia, fruit orchards crowd the banks and valleys of the Columbia's mid-Washington course.

The productivity of these regions defies description: When I calculated the number of boxcars required to ship the Yakima Valley's annual agricultural output, the imaginary train stretched from Yakima's downtown produce warehouses to Chicago.

bread on the shelves of a Polish market—a very real concern to millions of people, from the western rim of the Pacific to the Middle East. That might not be glamorous, but it is supremely important. "There are substitutes for oil," said Doug Urquhart of Lind, Washington, one of America's leading grain traders. "There are no substitutes for food."

Few dreamt of the wealth possible from the dry Northwest plains. The wagon trains of

Mask and goggles shield a wheat harvester near Ritzville, Washington, against the dust of a Mount St. Helens eruption. A choking nuisance, the ash in time enhances the soil.
FOLLOWING PAGES: *Giant wheels of farming fortune honeycomb the land near Boardman, Oregon. To irrigate the sandy terrain, pipes rotate over circles that measure half a mile across, sprinkling water from the Columbia. A decade earlier this cropland was desert.*

The Northwest in some ways seems more connected with its foreign customers than with the rest of the United States. Wheat and forest products make Portland the leading Pacific port for exports. Bentgrass seed grown in the Willamette is just as likely to re-sod a Scottish golf course as one in California. "We're a long way from the rest of the country by truck and rail," an Idaho shipper told me. "The Snake and the Columbia offer us cheap access to world markets. Export to the Chinese market promises to be our major trade in the coming years."

South of Idaho Falls I watched a maritime container on railroad tracks being loaded with potatoes for the South Pacific. The hot, dusty, treeless land stretched absolutely flat to the horizon. Few places look less suitable for agriculture, yet a few miles south, near the town of Shelley, I found the Harvard Bitter family entering its fourth generation of what Harvard calls "desert farming."

When I arrived, he and two of his four sons were bent over a seed-potato cutting machine that had jammed. Lance Bitter, 26, shook his head and walked out, muttering. Harvard spoke of windows, "the brief times you have to get things into your ground— seeds, fertilizer, herbicides—to achieve the maximum result. We need 120 growing days for a good crop of potatoes. When it rains too much, or when you have breakdowns like this, your troubles start to compound."

The Bitters farm 700 acres. Harvard's grandfather came from northern Utah in the early 1900s to farm the very plains dreaded by thirsty Oregon Trail migrants. "He lived to within six weeks of his 103rd birthday," Harvard recalled. "A testament to the benefits of hard work. Every day his family harnessed 80 head of plow horses. First drought and then the Depression of the 1930s got them. They walked off with what they could carry in a suitcase, found jobs for wages, rented a piece of ground, and started over. That's not an uncommon story around here."

A Mormon family, the Bitters number ten. Harvard flew bombers in the South Pacific during World War II and returned with a determination to establish himself. To do it, he has had to expand beyond his wildest expectations. "Shrinking profit margins force it," he told me. "I'd love to farm 40 acres and knock off at five, but that's a thing of history. We're dealing in big dollars, inflated dollars, huge fuel and electrical costs, and equipment prices that increase much faster than our prices do. To stay in farming you simply must expand, or get out. In our family we don't talk hours but rather in terms of what we can earn. If it takes 18 hours a day, that's what it takes. When the work gets heavy we eat and sleep in shifts. When we figure it out, we find ourselves working for half the minimum wage."

Such concerns seemed remote when I sat down to dinner with Harvard and his family. Throughout the afternoon grandchildren played on the dining room floor as Evada, Harvard's wife of 28 years, juggled household duties with church and community responsibilities. Daughters Myra and Lanae played crisp classical fugues on the living-room piano while Evada, an accomplished violinist who toured with the Brigham Young University Symphony, hummed along as she prepared the season's first garden greens. On the back patio, Lance shot baskets with brothers Kent, 23, and Greg, 10.

Supper was leisurely and congenial. Harvard watched the setting sun turn his fields gold. Then his attention returned to the table, and he smiled, a man who if burdened is nonetheless grateful to pursue his ambition.

I was directed to the Bitters by Russell N. Swensen, an agent for the University of Idaho Cooperative Extension Service in Bonneville

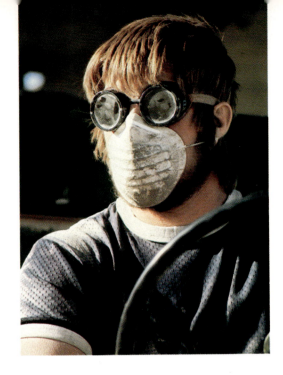

County. When I visited his office to inquire about the region's crops, his desk was covered with arcane brochures about nitrogen fertilizers, tillage methods, and the endocrinology of hogs. "That's farming," Russell said as I riffled through them. "This is challenging country to cultivate. You're fighting desert conditions." He held up more brochures, on the control of Rush skeletonweed, leafy spurge, potato leaf roll, and yellow starthistle. "The state and universities conduct the research that farmers haven't got the time or money to undertake. This academic effort is one big reason American farmers are the most productive in the world."

Probably no Northwest farm symbolizes the union of knowledge and sweat more than the cooperative community of the Warden Hutterian Brethren in the wheatlands near the Big Bend of the Columbia in Washington. "The ultimate farm," an admirer in Warden called it. "We strive toward excellence," said Jake Wollman, one of the community's leaders. "Excellence in anything is based on knowledge. We think we are about two or three years ahead of the trends."

Supper was ending for the community's 52 disciples of Joseph Hutter when I arrived. Like other Plain People, the Warden Hutterian Brethren dress according to tradition: dark pants, work shirts, and suspenders for the men; gingham dresses, aprons, and scarves for women. But the old-fashioned

ends there. "Our personal philosophies don't conflict with technology and private enterprise," said Eli Wollman, patriarch of the Wollman clan, reclining in an armchair built in the Brethren's cabinet shop. A rolltop desk built on special commission sold for $10,000. Its mate, big as an ox, took up half of Eli's living room wall. I felt of its finish, smooth as glass. "Not a nail in it," said Eli proudly, "All dovetails fit together."

The community's residences, built to the same standards as Eli's desk, stand on a manicured lawn surrounded by 10,000 acres of wheat and other crops. Inside concrete buildings as large as commercial airplane hangars, state-of-the-art farm machines, polished like fire engines, were parked in precise rows.

One building held a full repair and maintenance shop. In his basement, Jake, Jr., and a friend were soldering the circuits of a home-built computer designed to monitor the farm's use of power and water through a network of remote sensors.

The Brethren also engage in dry farming similar to that of the Palouse wheatlands to the east. The sparsely settled, three-million-acre Palouse country covers part of the Columbia Plateau, with Spokane the only major city. Dry and windswept, among the youngest of America's agricultural areas, the Palouse today accounts for 10 percent of the nation's soft, white, winter wheat crop, which is used mainly for pasta. Most of it is raised without irrigation to supplement the 14 to 22 inches of annual rainfall. Dry farming yields 35 to more than 100 bushels an acre. For those willing to bear the enormous investments required to wring a bushel from this hilly plain, the contours of which resemble an ocean with mile-long swells rising hundreds of feet, the rewards can be large.

The Hutterian people moved to the Warden area from southern Alberta in 1956,

For a good life and sweet land: The Harvard Bitters give thanks for hard-earned crops of potatoes, wheat, and barley. Fourth-generation farmers, the Bitters work 18-hour days in the spring to irrigate their 700 acres with Snake River waters near Shelley, Idaho.

owned their 10,000 acres by 1970, and began building in 1972. They are now involved in a joint venture with another community 17 miles away. "You see what people can do if they cooperate," Jake declared.

The 12 schoolchildren in the community study in the Brethren's schoolhouse; they are taught by an accredited teacher. Tested against all students in Washington, they achieved superior levels. "We respect achievement," Jake told me. "The kids start working at 16. They choose their area of work according to their abilities and interests, and our needs. We work together, we innovate,

and we roll with the future. The challenge is to do things better, always better."

That might well be the motto of 75-year-old Grady Auvil, whose achievements as an apple grower north of Wenatchee are world famous. Grady defied most of the rules of his trade, and after some 16 years of work, has become the leading grower of the Granny Smith, a green, bruise-resistant apple with a piquant taste and a long shelf life, probably destined to become one of the most popular apples in America. Auvil holds patents on two strains of the Granny Smith.

"I just like to have fun and make bucks."

The planting's done: Harvard Bitter stands before his field; straight furrows cut between rows of potato hills.

He laughed as he told me of his experiments. While he talked, he made me a cup of coffee in 11 seconds. "I like to do things well and quickly," he said. "That's the process of improving life."

Grady has vastly improved the process of growing apples. Conventional wisdom held that 270 trees per acre was optimum. Grady doubled that using dwarf trees with early bearing habits onto which he grafted Granny Smith shoots. "American buyers were importing them from New Zealand, Chile, France, Argentina, and South Africa, and we weren't even growing them here! This is the easiest country in the world to grow fruit, here on the river. It was crazy." While most new orchards took eight years to mature, Grady's crowded dwarfs, held up straight by plastic twine, paid for the annual operating costs in two. "The third leaf made a profit. In five years, the investment, about $10,000 an acre, was returned. Fun. Bucks."

Grady and Lillie Auvil live in a bright, airy ranch-style home overlooking the Columbia. Grady's son and daughter participate in the business, but the Auvil operation far exceeds family dimensions. "I only have one ambition," said Grady as we bounced through the orchards in his station wagon. "That's to build a farm organization that endures beyond me. To accomplish that I knew I had to go outside of family. I like to see people progress, so we've made it a policy to stimulate the people who work for us to better themselves and take responsibility by offering a financial participation in the business."

When the Columbia was dammed at Rocky Reach below the Auvil orchards, Grady anticipated the loss of 80 vertical feet of land and raced to reshape his new waterfront in advance of rising backwaters. "We were shoving dirt around 24 hours a day during the last year and a half," he recalled. The result was a campground for workers and the hordes of young farmers and agronomists who come from around the world to learn, and a swimming lagoon. "You gotta have fun in life," Grady reflected, shoving a Boston Pops cassette into his car stereo. "These dwarf trees on double rows are going to add a thousand boxes an acre to normal yields. That's fun." At $17 a box, I calculated, $17,000 worth of fun per acre. "I've never been so excited about growing apples," said Grady, whose apples are marketed under an appropriate trade name, "Gee Whiz."

The wind was gusting when I drove south from the Auvil orchards. I crossed the Columbia at Vantage in a hot gale. The air seemed filled with white smoke—residual ash from the eruption of Mount St. Helens a year before. A colossal inconvenience to Northwesterners in the path of the volcano's huge cloud of ash, in geologic terms it was merely a replenishment of an important ingredient of the region's astonishing fertility.

Scientists credit earlier volcanic explosions with the ashfall that contributed to the high mineral content of Yakima Valley soils. Today that alluvial valley, two adjacent basins flanking the Yakima River, is one of the major fruit- and vegetable-growing centers in the country. It's best known for Delicious apples, mint oil—the flavoring ingredient in candies and toothpastes—and hops, the yellowish flowers plucked from vines for their extract, which imparts the bitter aromatic taste to beer.

Roughly three-fourths of America's hop harvest comes from Washington, and all of that from the Yakima Valley's 31,000 acres of vines. The Yakima crop is second only to the entire output of Germany, the world's leading producer. About half is exported. It is one of the small curiosities of an increasingly interdependent world that some of the finest imported beers available in America owe their flavors in part to the Yakima hop.

When I visited the fields in late May, I found workers busy winding new vines around the twines that would support their growth. Most of the workers are migrants who hope for six months of reasonably steady work as pickers, tree pruners, ditchdiggers, and equipment operators.

"We earned $13,000 last year," said W. T. Hall. A Missouri-born migrant, father of four, he fought to restrain his pet raccoon in his lap as we talked in the shade of his 21-foot trailer near Granger. He and his wife, Ardena, make their home in a succession of trailer courts from Florida to Washington.

W. T.'s father went on the road during the Dust Bowl years. His children are the third generation of Halls adrift on the rural landscape. "Best pay's here in Washington, picking apples at eight bucks a bin. We fill about 20 a day." Starting at dawn, W. T. and Ardena work until midafternoon with Robert, 19, and June, 17. After six weeks, working six days a week, they had earned about $4,800. Last year their gasoline costs exceeded $1,500 for their 11,000-mile odyssey. The two youngest children, aged 9 and 7, stay with an aunt and attend school in the Ozarks.

"There's no future in this," W. T. told me. "Robert's thinking about joining the Army. June's looking for steady work in Yakima. The important thing is to keep the youngest in school. It's not good for a family to split up, but there's nothing for the boys out here." And, he said, his family faced increasing competition from Mexican families "screaming for work at any pay. It's a real mess, but here's still the best work there is. We want to retire with our kids all off the road. That's our goal."

Of the estimated 30,000 agricultural workers who flood the valley every year, fed-eral immigration officials believe that at least 10,000 are Mexican nationals without work visas—"illegals," in local jargon, the perennial "wetbacks" of a long and dreary search for a decent living. Some Northwest growers candidly admit that without this supplemental work force, the industry would collapse. While the federal government strives for a solution, other agencies monitor the fields for abuses and try to bring basic services to these workers, both legal and illegal.

"We need them," said grower Dan McDonald. "There's work for everyone and, while it's hard, the wages around here are generous." Dan and Mildred McDonald's hopyards, northeast of Wapato, date from 1877, two years after the first commercial harvest. Around that time a pound of dried hop flowers brought 85 cents. In 1975 the price was 81 cents. "We just had to become more efficient," Dan told me. "We had organized our industry—hired agents to check worldwide supply and demand, and began to advertise. It worked until 1979 when inflation finally overtook us."

Freeway construction claimed 100 of the McDonalds' 180 acres of vines, land that had been in hop production for 85 years; so the McDonalds went across the river and leased 100 acres of Yakima Indian land. Dan and I lunched at the Heritage Inn restaurant, part of the new cultural center at the Yakima Nation's 1.4-million-acre reservation.

In early August the valley's hop fraternity holds a pint-size Oktoberfest in Moxee City, where growers and their friends celebrate the coming harvest, and rue prices and the scourge of aphids while drinking beer flavored with their crops.

Like many Northwestern farmers, Dan pursues large-scale recreations and formidable projects. When highway planners aimed their pavement through his vintage hop dryer,

"Central Washington has the finest climate in the world for growing fruit," says apple baron Grady Auvil, perched on a battered command car above his orchards along the Columbia. He ranks as the leading producer of Granny Smiths. This green apple, Auvil says, originated some 115 years ago when an Australian woman threw out apple cores along a creek. From them mutants grew—and the fruit took Granny's name.

a multi-story building, Dan moved it aside for preservation as a kind of family museum. "Our concern," he said, "is focused on preserving private agriculture. Many farm wives are active in Women For The Survival of Agriculture, which has been instrumental in modifying the inheritance tax laws which have been a killer of family-held farms. . . . It's not only from sentiment that I believe the family farm is important to this country. It's a most productive and efficient sector of our economy, and it's a barometer of individual enterprise. If we go out of business, there's serious trouble ahead for all Americans."

The admonition isn't new, but it was not until the last decade that a general alarm alerted Northwesterners to the weakening of a major economic base. Much credit must go to the Oregon farmers whose main concern was and still is the Willamette Valley in which lie 2.7 million acres of the state's finest farmland. The problem: people. "It's a common paradox of American life," said a city planner in Eugene. "The valley is a beautiful place where everyone wants to live. It's easily subdivided. The farmers have cleared and leveled the land. So urbanites come to fill the housing developments. Others buy small parcels of land once under cultivation—ranchettes, we call them unsympathetically. Farmland is reduced, prices soar, and the qualities that attracted these new residents in the first place are erased."

Nearly 1.8 million people live in the valley today. By the year 2000, a population of 2.3 million is expected. Land purchased a generation ago for $500 an acre now may command up to $10,000—a windfall to sellers, but a giant obstacle to a new generation of farmers. *(Continued on page 137)*

Home is where the harvest is for the migrant workers who journey north to pick Washington's produce each year. At a Wenatchee district orchard a worker (right) fills a shoulder-slung, bushel-size canvas sack with Red Delicious. Some migrants found a home in company cabins during the six-week apple-picking season. When cabins filled up, the grower's sign pointed the way to campground housing. Migrant labor, most growers believe, ensures a successful harvest.

Pert young sprout cuts asparagus on a Sunnyside farm in the Yakima Valley. Across the field, a Mexican-American family (below) fills lugs with fresh spears for transport to a packing shed,

where the adults will finish their working day. During the spring asparagus harvest, children help their parents with the cutting, then catch the bus to school— earning an education that helps them and their families adjust to a permanent life in the United States. The Yakima region lures new residents with the promise of the irrigated valley—half a million acres of fruits and vegetables, a cropland cradled between the Columbia River and the Cascades. In addition to some 13,000 acres of asparagus, the Yakima country supplies a sixth of the nation's apples and three-fourths of its hops.

Soil and sun have done their work, and summer's vine-tending has ended; now the clusters of the noble Chardonnay head for the vats at Tualatin Vineyards in the Willamette Valley—

and more months of intensive care. Vintners here chose a setting in the lee of the Coast Range to grow classic grapes in a climate similar to that of famous European wine regions.

Serene farmscapes patch the southern Willamette—an uncrowded scene that Oregonians hope to preserve. New state laws help curb urban growth in a 115-mile stretch of the valley, prized for farming and home to 70 percent of Oregon's population.

Ken Kesey, an Oregonian since boyhood and author of *One Flew Over the Cuckoo's Nest,* also engages in farming. Years ago, when he joined with others seeking a grass-roots determination of political priorities for the state, the preservation of its farmland placed among the highest.

"Take our place," Ken said. "Seventy acres in all, 50 in hay. Last year we brought in 4,800 bales. But that isn't a living. I have other income, but what about all the old-time farmers on small places who don't? There are changes taking place that aren't in the best interests of this country's agriculture."

It was nearing hay harvest when I drove along country roads to Ken and Faye Kesey's Pleasant Hill farm. The afternoon was somnolent, heavy with the scent of wild herbs and flowers, the sun hot, the air still. "When the harvest begins around here," Ken told me, "the whole valley is galvanized into one. For two to three weeks, maybe a month, that's the only thing on your mind. We loan each other equipment we can't afford to buy, and it draws the neighborhood together like nothing I know of but sports. We've talked about turning it into a hay Olympics."

Like many small family farms, the Kesey spread bears the stamp of its owners' personalities. There are berry patches, a fish pond, Ken's shed-office, a large hex sign on the roof peak of the house, which is in fact a converted barn. Beef cattle graze the pasture and there are chickens, some of which enjoy the safer status of household pets if not the admiration accorded the family peacocks.

"Farm life demands attention to a lot of details," Ken observed, "but time flows smoothly. Events sort of ooze from one to another. You can think, and make a world more to your liking." If many Willamette Valley farmers had their way, there would be boundaries beyond which developers could not build. Such laws exist but are complex and subject to constant challenge. The retention of agricultural land was the main reason for the creation of Oregon's Land Conservation and Development Commission.

In Eugene photographer Bob Madden and I studied an official computer-generated map of the city's urban boundary, a supposed barrier to new urban development. We took a helicopter to compare policy with reality. For the most part they conformed, but in at least one boundary area where the map showed farmland, paved streets awaited the building of a subdivision. North of town, the interstate highway cut through the fields of an old farm.

"It sure chopped our place up," said 33-year-old Walter Johnson, who operates a popular open-air fruit and produce market in his farmyard. "They paid my grandparents three times market value, but in the long run, the state got a better deal."

Walter's grandfather bought 30 acres by the Johnsons' fruit stand in 1915, cleared the thick stands of ash, oak, maple, and cottonwood using dynamite and horses, and wholesaled his produce in a downtown market until 1959. "Loyal customers followed us out to the farm when the market shut down," said Walter. Two of his brothers pursue small-scale organic farming; Walter and his wife, Sandra, work 150 acres of wheat, 33 acres of sugar beet seed, 200 acres of row crops, 30 acres of mint, and 20 acres of berries.

We drove along in Walter's truck, over his beet field, then stopped at the fruit stand to see how business was going. At the family's public strawberry field, local residents were picking their own fruit as trucks hurtled by on the freeway 70 feet away.

We walked the field behind Walter's home to check the effectiveness of an herbicide, adjusted the air flow through the family greenhouse where seedlings are nurtured, then spent a quarter hour helping Sandra pull weeds from their front-yard flower bed.

"This is an occupation where it takes two," said Sandra. "For the farm to succeed, a farm wife has to be involved. There's so much stress, so many decisions to be made." During harvests Sandra drives trucks to market, and throughout the year works at the vegetable stand and keeps the account books and payroll. "We met in college," she told me. "I was completely enamored by the farm, the life, watching things grow. I enjoy being around farmers. They're honest and they say what they mean."

"I got a degree in psychology," Walter said, "with the intention of becoming a psychoanalyst. But my mother didn't have anyone to help her aggressively manage the farm, and my brothers and sisters were still too young, so I came back."

More often than not these days, the people who till the fertile valleys, wheatlands, and desert farms are carrying on a family tradition that borders on a private obsession. "When you work soil your parents and their parents before them gave their hearts to," said Harrisburg seed grower John Hayworth, "it's much more than simply business."

The human traditions of the Northwest's agrarian society are renewed each year in a series of celebrations like the Yakima Valley's hop-growers' festival. I joined hundreds of people on a June day for the Strawberry Festival at Lebanon, Oregon, and helped to consume what was billed as the world's largest strawberry shortcake, a concoction bigger than most automobiles—big enough to make 17,000 portions.

Though draft horses were replaced long ago by tractors, the massive Scottish Clydesdales, French Percherons, and broad-shouldered Belgians that broke the Northwest soil are still treasured by the region's horse enthusiasts. Some still work, dragging logs from forests undergoing selective cutting, but their exertions today are mostly ceremonial. Harnessed into teams, they compete every summer in Eugene, demonstrating their awesome pulling power as buyers bid great sums for them.

Watching two four-horse teams claw the turf in a snorting tug-of-war, I noticed that almost everyone around me wore jogging shoes. In Eugene, sports and physical fitness are a civic mania, and the area's sprinters and distance runners have competed in Olympic and other major track events for years. The city is traversed by jogging paths and bicycle lanes. Eugene is a bicycle town; its central mall is reserved for pedestrians.

"A human-engineered city," commented a city planner, locking his lightweight racer to a rack after his 4½-mile ride to work. "The quality of life is on the minds of

"Driving back, we passed a series of pastoral scenes: dairy cows grazing lush fields, old moss-encrusted rail fences, quiet fish ponds, and roadside assemblies of barnyard chickens. The fields buzzed with insects. The valley was hushed. 'Tualatin is Indian for "slow and easy-flowing,"' said Bill. 'Appropriate name, isn't it?'"

many urban Oregonians, particularly here. They want their air and water clean. They want their health protected, and they want a say in how that gets accomplished."

The passage of Oregon's famed law banning the sale of pull-top beverage cans, and the cleanup of the polluted Willamette River, both results of concerted civic action, signaled a renewal during the past decade of grass-roots political activism in the state. "People's concerns have a way of becoming law here," a Salem lawyer remarked. Take the case of Oregon's emerging winemakers. Frustrated by labeling regulations in other states that obscured the origins and composition of competing wines, they wrote and got passed one of the nation's strictest consumer-oriented labeling laws.

"We're willing to stand by our own names and locations," said Bill Fuller, the winemaster and a founder of the prizewinning Tualatin Vineyards near Forest Grove. "We outlawed all the names that emulate a European wine region, like Chablis, Burgundy, and Rhine. Our wines must carry labels identifying the region of their origin, and the grapes used to make them. We're not making Rhine wines; we're making Oregon wines, which are world-class wines—even though when I go on the road to sell, I spend half my time telling them where Oregon is."

Trained in enology and food science at the University of California's Davis campus, Bill was working at a Napa Valley winery when he met Bill Malkmus, a California banker who became his partner. They decided to make wines "someplace unusual and different," Bill Fuller said. "We considered the north coasts of California and Oregon, eliminating unlivable places, excessively expensive places, and places too remote. A state nursery inspector suggested this site, and it has far exceeded even our best hopes."

Working mostly by themselves, Bill and his wife, Virginia, started in 1973 with a spring planting of Riesling, Chardonnay, Pinot Noir, and Gewurztraminer grapes.

I sat in the kitchen of Bill and Virginia's Victorian-style hilltop house and sampled a white Riesling and a pink-hued Pinot Noir blanc. "Oregon wines have a unique taste," Bill noted. "Regional winemakers strive for the ultimate quality possible from a suitable location, which of course you select in the

hope it will produce superior wines. Some Northwest wines really can't be compared save against themselves, while others can compete internationally."

Outside, the buds on the vines were breaking open, and vineyard workers were spraying sulfur to prevent mildew. Bill summed up for me the rounds of the vintner's seasons: "You have to train the shoots, and then with summer there's trimming and topping to do. The harvest comes with the autumn, and then in winter we prune back the vines. Bottling starts in early spring. We're producing about 40,000 gallons a year now."

We drove down through the Tualatin Valley—whose river joins the Willamette—toward Forest Grove to pick up Bill's teenage daughter Denise at the library. The Fullers' house commands a bucolic view of forest, orchard, and field, most of the orchards given to filbert trees. Virtually the entire American crop is grown in the Willamette Valley. "It's always peaceful around here," said Bill, "except in rainy Octobers when they use the downdrafts of hovering helicopters to blow the nuts from the trees."

With some four feet of rain a year, the northern reach of the Willamette Valley is thickly overgrown with wild grass and berry bushes that drooped down over the back roads we traveled. Driving back, we passed a series of pastoral scenes: dairy cows grazing lush fields, old moss-encrusted rail fences, quiet fish ponds, and roadside assemblies of barnyard chickens. The fields buzzed with insects. The valley was hushed. "Tualatin is Indian for 'slow and easy-flowing,' " said Bill. "Appropriate name, isn't it?"

Before I had to leave, we enjoyed a final toast. I remarked that it was splendid stuff. "That's Oregon," Bill smiled. We clinked our glasses to the fortunes of future Northwest harvests, and said good-bye.

Past forested slopes veiled in haze, a tug pushes barges up the Columbia River Gorge. Cutting a 75-mile-long swath through the Cascade Range, this idyllic passage gives little hint of the workaday power of the mighty waterway, economic lifeline of the Northwest.

The Columbia

By Bill Richards

The million-dollar button sits glowing but untouched in a locked, cavernous room under a hillside in the busy port of Vancouver, Washington. Although it has never been pushed, the button is a small but instructive component in the endlessly complicated relationship between the Northwest and the Columbia River.

"Push that button," Charlie Brown said, pointing to the electronic console blinking at us, "and the ten biggest industrial energy consumers in the Northwest have just five minutes to drop half their power load."

Flashing the cutoff signal would be the last and most dramatic step, Charlie explained, if his employer, the Bonneville Power Administration, suddenly had a critical drop in hydroelectrical or thermal-generated power. The BPA gathers and distributes the power from 32 federal dams and three thermal plants along the Columbia River system. A cutoff could idle thousands of workers from Montana to the Pacific; nearly a third of the nation's aluminum smelters might have to cut production by half. No wonder, I thought, that Charlie and the people who operate the BPA's Dittmer Control Center here call it the million-dollar button.

Ultimately the decision on whether to push the button or not depends on the river system. Imagine a machine capable of making six million acres of desert spring to life, of providing contemporary comforts for millions of people in seven states, of carrying more than 45 million tons of cargo on its waters every year, and all the while providing a habitat for countless fish. The Columbia River system does all these things. The Columbia is truly a river of miracles.

But it is more than just a machine, no matter how the dam builders have worked to break and tame it. I made that discovery as I traveled the 745-mile course from the misty, evergreen-lined riverbank near the Pacific Coast, through the twisting canyons of Oregon and the deserts of Washington, to the highlands along the Canadian border. The Columbia, I found, is a river of both strengths and weaknesses.

And secrets. Such as the bald eagles' nests hidden among the sloughs of a cluster of low-lying islands; I came upon them near the river mouth in the pewter light of a rainy May morning. Or the rickety fishing platforms balanced high on the walls of a narrow canyon just off the Columbia Gorge; there I watched Indians perform a graceful ballet as they dipped long-handled nets for Chinook salmon, just as their ancestors did before the first Europeans came to the river nearly two centuries ago. The secrets include gold, washed down from the mountains far to the north and available to those who know the river well enough to look in the right places.

But that is jumping ahead too fast. To begin to know the Columbia, I found, one should start at its mouth, with a guide like Bob Ziak.

Nearly everyone in Clatsop County, Oregon, calls Bob by the nickname "Kewpie." "The nurse held me up when I was born and said 'Doesn't he look just like a Kewpie doll.' I guess the name stuck," he told me, comfortable with it after 64 years.

A logger by trade, Kewpie Ziak certainly doesn't look like his tiny namesake now. He is a stocky, broad-shouldered man with a quick-fuse temper easily aroused by any threat to his beloved Columbia. I first heard of him a few years ago when he helped organize opposition to plans for an aluminum smelter along the lower Columbia. The site lay near the spot the explorers Meriwether Lewis and William Clark had praised as "a butifull Sand Shore." Facing a buzz saw of opposition, the plans never materialized.

Splashing down the Canadian Rockies, winding through central Washington, then bending westward to border Oregon, the Columbia River flows 1,214 miles before spilling into the Pacific near Astoria. Along its way it drops more than 2,500 feet. As the result of extensive damming since the 1930s, a staircase of quiet lakes lines the river where rapids once boiled. Harnessing the Columbia's energy transformed this relatively undeveloped corner of the country into a land of plenty. Cheap hydroelectric power sparked the growth of towns and industries. Water pumped from reservoirs turned scrubland into farmland, and canals skirting the dams paved a highway of commerce for the bounty of the Northwest.

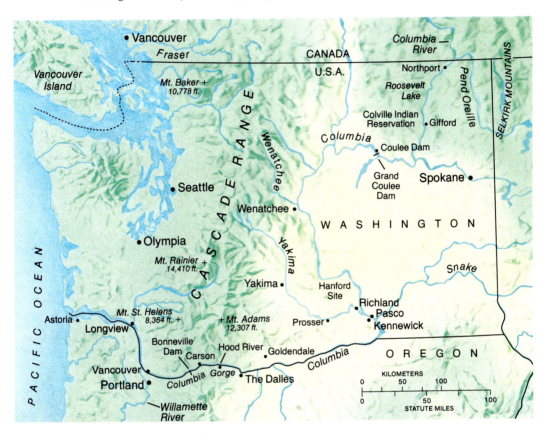

"There's no one raised along this river without it becoming a part of him," Kewpie shouted as he and his brother Gary nosed a small boat through the rain into the five-mile-wide Columbia estuary. Kewpie bellowed out the landmarks with a voice that would be clearly audible over any falling tree.

"This river is a magnet," he said. "It's a different world. It's not just beautiful, it's an adventure." The river here lives up to that billing admirably. It flows by banks covered with maples, hemlocks, spruces, and Douglas firs that loom nearly black in the raw light of early morning. It carves quiet coves and backwaters where weekend adventurers occasionally turn up the remains of Indian fishing camps, long abandoned and forgotten under clusters of huckleberry bushes.

Along the banks blue herons sit staring down from their treetop nests; their eyes look angry. A lone outboard sputters past, towing its catch—a 70-foot cedar log, a victim, perhaps, of Mount St. Helens miles upstream. Along the rocky outcrops, marked by the rise and fall of tides, lichens and mosses compose natural murals, as outlandish and colorful as any man-made abstract art.

Nearly 160 species of birds were spotted during a count made in two wildlife refuges along the lower Columbia in the 1970s. Gary claims one that didn't get counted—"a snowy owl we found after they left."

Like ruins of an ancient civilization, columns of basalt crumble beside the Columbia. Wild flowers and lichens brighten the sun-burnished rock in the river's gorge. About 16 million years ago lava pouring from cracks in the earth flowed down the ancestral Columbia Valley. As the lava cooled and solidified into rock, shrinkage caused it to break off at right angles, creating this and other natural colonnades along the riverbanks.

There is a deceptive sluggishness to a big river like the Columbia. It passes Astoria and heads toward the open Pacific at about four knots. But the ebb and flow of the waters can swing the huge seagoing ships anchored off Astoria's piers as if they were bathtub toys.

The forces meeting over the Columbia bar—the river's flow and the ocean tides—are awesome. At least 2,000 vessels have perished around the mouth of the river; more than 1,500 lives have been lost.

Yet when Capt. Robert Gray swung his ship, the *Columbia Rediviva,* across the bar on a cloudy May morning in 1792 he recorded his discovery of the fabled "River of the West" in his log with little fanfare.

"We found this to be a large river of fresh water, up which we steered," this Yankee master of understatement wrote. "Vast numbers of natives came alongside." Gray did a little trading—and sailed out of the pages of history with barely another word. But the river bears his ship's name, and his discoveries gave America a claim to the Northwest.

I prefer another account of the Columbia that was given at 6 a. m. on October 25, 1906, by a shaken ship's captain as he sat on a beached log just outside the river mouth. He had been waiting on his ship, the British bark *Peter Iredale,* just off the bar for some morning light to steer across, the captain said. A southeasterly gale and a heavy current wrenched the ship out of the control of its 20-man crew and heaved it toward the beach.

The first shock sent the mizzenmast overboard, said the captain, "and when she struck again, parts of other masts snapped like pipe stems." He pronounced it "a miracle" that he and his crew had survived.

I went to see the wreckage of the *Peter Iredale.* It rests a few miles from the mouth of the Columbia, a half-buried hulk with rust holes in its iron hull, a landmark and a warning for those who would take the power of the river and the sea too lightly.

But when I headed upriver the next day on the Korean freighter *Pan Ivory,* the Columbia suddenly didn't seem so big. In fact, with 482 feet of ship churning under us, the river appeared alarmingly narrow.

"You certainly get a different perspective of the river from up here," Capt. Mitch Boyce said, keeping an eye on the ship headed downriver toward us. Mitch, at 35, was the youngest of the 41 members of the Columbia River Pilots Association. The pilots moved 2,239 vessels up and down the river in 1980, some of them in the thousand-foot supertanker class, making the Columbia River system the second busiest for shipping in the nation, after the Mississippi.

No ship captain today navigates his own vessel up the Columbia. The channel twists and turns the full length of its 101-mile passage to Portland. Pilots say they change course about a hundred times during the trip, just to match the river's meanderings. Mount St. Helens further complicated matters when it erupted in 1980, dumping a ledge of volcanic silt across the channel.

Then there are the fogs. Mitch has navigated the entire Portland passage by radar without once getting a look at the shoreline. "It's all up here anyway, the whole river," he said, tapping the side of his head.

I mentioned as casually as I could that the downriver ship now seemed headed right at us. Mitch nodded. "We only have a 600-foot-wide channel," he said, "and when you meet another ship the correct thing to do is aim at each other and veer off at the last minute." I watched, with visions of our cargo bobbing through a hole in the *Pan Ivory's* side, but the maneuver was executed smoothly. Both ships' pilots waved as they passed, filling the Columbia Valley with the

*"I have so enjoyed this world around me
that I find it is not only my desire but my
responsibility to help save it for generations
to come," says Bob "Kewpie" Ziak, a logger
and lifelong resident of the lower Columbia.
With this purpose at heart, Ziak fights for
his endangered neighbors. He rallied support
to halt logging that would have destroyed
the nest site of bald eagles near the river.
An eagle swoops by (opposite), beak agape.*

echoes of their whistles. Closer to Vancouver, on the Washington side, where we were scheduled to dock, the riverbank becomes cluttered with industry. More than 85 percent of the Northwest's wheat exports move through grain elevators along the lower Columbia. At Longview, Washington, the Weyerhaeuser Company's forest-products manufacturing complex, one of the biggest in the world, takes up more than a mile of riverfront. Alcoa's huge aluminum smelter spreads along the river in Vancouver. And Portland is the biggest exporting port in the West. The Columbia was obviously a busy river as Mitch slipped the *Pan Ivory* alongside its pier with about as much fuss as parking a Buick. Safely berthed, we hitched a ride on a tug headed a short way up the nearby Willamette River to Portland.

No city revels in its "livability" the way Portland does. Ask someone from New York or Los Angeles about those towns and you are likely to get a burst of crime statistics. Portlanders describe their city in terms of miles of parkland and jogging paths. It does have more rainy days than most cities, but its inhabitants don't seem to mind an average 150 days of misty weather each year. The rain combines with a mild and lengthy growing season to nurture spectacular gardens. Portlanders garden with a passion; reputedly, they have formed more garden clubs per capita than any other city in the country. Portland's rose society boasts that it is the country's oldest and largest; the city's International Rose Test Garden flames each spring with nearly 10,000 plants of 400 varieties. Even the police cars flaunt a rose on their doors.

And how many cities have a formal Japanese garden overlooking the downtown business district, its silence broken only by the hushing of the wind in the surrounding firs? A former Portland mayor once proposed, quite

seriously, that every other residential street in the city be vacated and the occupants replaced with shade trees and roses.

There is almost a smugness about it all, and when I showed Portland Mayor Frank

"No city revels in its 'livability' the way Portland does. . . . Portlanders describe their city in terms of miles of parkland and jogging paths. It does have more rainy days than most cities, but its inhabitants don't seem to mind. . . . The rain combines with a mild and lengthy growing season to nurture spectacular gardens."

Ivancie a newspaper story critical of his city, he seemed taken aback.

"Most Livable City?" the headline asked.

The story talked about racism, corruption, and dirty air in Portland. One federal study even ranked Portland's air quality below Detroit's. "They like to pick on us because we are the best," said the mayor. "Portland is like a good-looking woman. Sure there are flaws, but she doesn't really change; her beauty lasts."

It is true that Portland has had the same sort of urban problems that any city of 365,000 might expect; but the mayor's point that his city is a benchmark for standards of gracious urban living is also true. Where else would you find graceful, bronze fountains bubbling on downtown street corners? Lumber baron Simon Benson had them built, it is said, to give his lumberjacks a natural alternative to the harder refreshments available to them in Portland's bars.

Walking around Portland I found it hard to believe that less than a century ago this was considered among the most evil and dangerous cities in the Far West. So notorious were its riverfront bars, alleys, and dives that a

federal investigation was launched around 1900 after complaints from the governments of England, France, and Germany that the port was not safe for their sailors.

The Portland waterfront in the 19th century abounded with "crimps," men who shanghaied the unwary to fill the crews for the ships in foreign trade that tied up here. The most famous crimp of them all was one Joseph "Bunco" Kelly. On one occasion he discovered 24 men lying dead or dying in a waterfront cellar after they drank formaldehyde, mistaking it for a keg of liquor. Trundling the bodies aboard an outbound ship, the crimp collected $720 from the captain, assuring him that his expired crewmen would sleep off their stupor and be fit for duty on the high seas in the morning.

Some Portlanders have a tendency to overlook this seamy side of their city's history—but not Bill Naito, a Portland native whose development firm is busily renovating the once down-at-heels waterfront area, now called Old Town.

"This was once a wide open place, but it was never really seedy," Bill said, as we sat one morning in his office in an old warehouse. "The mayor and the city's leading businessmen drank here, side by side with loggers, railroad men, and seamen."

Well, not exactly side by side, I discovered, as I poked through an empty Old Town building after borrowing the key from Bill. A 684-foot-long bar—claimed as the world's longest—once stood in this structure. The saloon was called Erickson's; it had 50 bartenders, a pipe organ, a 300-pound bouncer, and a corner set aside just for visiting Russian seamen. Workingmen drank on the main floor, while the city's upper crust—Bill Naito calls them "the coattails"—sat on a balcony overlooking the carousing throng. Prostitutes did their work in back *(Continued on page 162)*

Foreign exchange: Northwestern forests depart, Toyotas roll in. Ships bound for Japan fill their holds and pile their decks with logs at the huge Weyerhaeuser Company complex at Longview, Washington. About a third of the logs harvested in the state go into the export trade—most of them to Japan. Reflecting the trend, a freighter flying the flag of this major trading partner bears the name of the ship's westbound cargoes. Traffic from Japan brings mainly finished products to the Northwest. A worker (below) helps unload the imports at the Port of Portland.

Everything's coming up roses in Portland, and each spring the city celebrates with a lavish Rose Festival, a tradition since 1907. Highlighting ten days of events, the Grand Floral Parade glides through downtown in a flotilla of fantasy. This creation won a Royal Rosarian Trophy. Although official judging takes place before the parade, spectators may offer unofficial judgments (left) as the entries pass by. With mild temperatures and frequent watering—the city averages 150 rainy days annually—flowers bloom here year round. Located a hundred miles inland near the confluence of the Willamette and the Columbia Rivers, Portland ranks as the largest city in the Columbia system and, despite its distance from the sea, one of the busiest Pacific Coast ports.

Nestled in the soothing surroundings of the Columbia Gorge, Carson Hot Springs Resort has drawn people to its mineral baths since 1876, when the St. Martins, an Indian family, discovered thermal waters and built a spa. Restored and modernized, the original hotel (right) remains as a landmark, a reminder of days when patrons came by riverboat and by buggy. Guests still soak in mineral water at 126°F, then lie wrapped in blankets that lock in the heat. Henry Kolbaba, at right, an arthritis patient and live-in patron of 88, takes the waters several times a week.

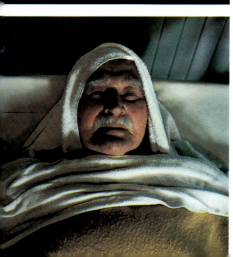

Kindled by sunlight, space-age windmills stand ready to seize the wind and churn it into electricity. The Boeing Company built these giant turbines for the federal government as an experiment in wind power. Each steel blade measures 150 feet long; painters apply a fresh coat

with the help of a crane hoist. With dependable wind speeds of 14 to 45 miles an hour, the three computerized windmills can generate enough power for a town of 3,000. Engineers envision a windmill farm of a hundred or more whirling turbines on this blustery hilltop near Goldendale, Washington, and on windswept fields all over the Northwest. FOLLOWING PAGES: Farther upriver the quest for energy continues at the Hanford nuclear reservation. Climbing a lattice of steel rods, a worker checks the welds at one of three nuclear power plants in various stages of construction.

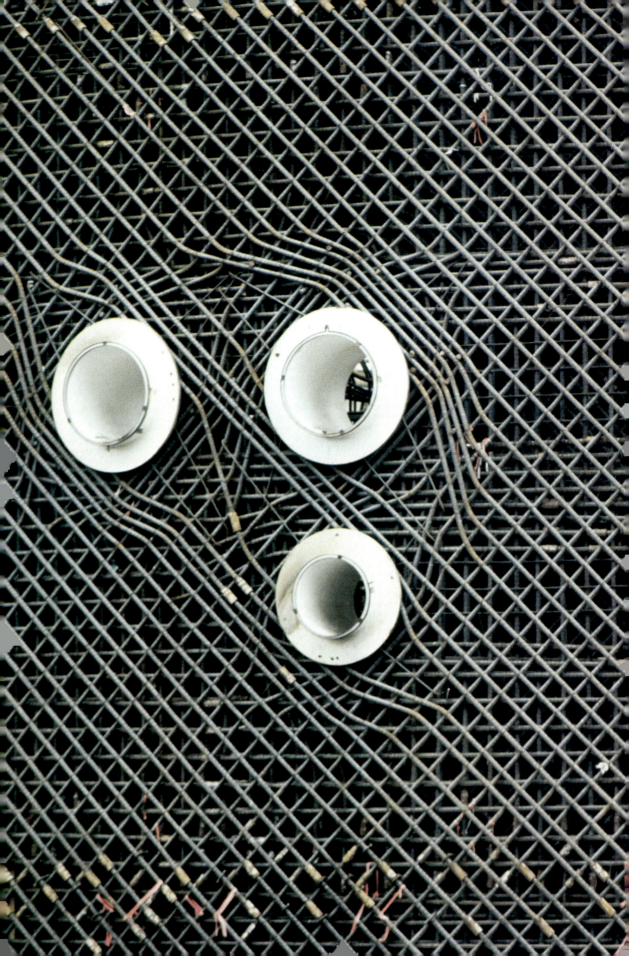

Machinery of the nuclear age rises along the Columbia at the Hanford works. Reactors here have produced plutonium since 1944, when the federal government selected this isolated 570-square-mile site in central Washington for secret research on the atom bomb. In the satellite community of Richland, even the nickname of the Columbia High School football team recalls the area's pioneering role in the development of nuclear power. Today only one reactor operates at Hanford, the dual-purpose N Reactor, which supplies plutonium for the military and steam to generate electricity for Northwest utilities. A treatment facility for radioactive wastes zigzags away from the buildings. In the distance stand the ghostly stacks of reactors long since shut down yet still dangerously radioactive. Harold "Mac" McCluskey (right), a former employee at Hanford, exhibits his own levels of radiation. Wearing dark glasses to shield his light-sensitive eyes, he uses a gamma counter to measure the radioactivity still in his body. During a chemical explosion in 1976 he sustained the largest internal dose of radiation on record for nuclear workers.

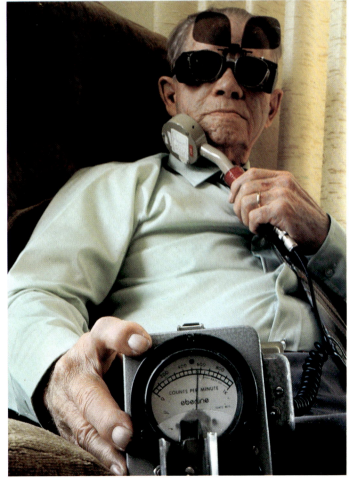

Signals light up a control panel in a check of warning systems at a nuclear power plant at Hanford.

rooms, in stalls called cribs. Men too drunk to resist fell prey to the crimps.

Portland today is certainly less raucous, but it is still tied closely to the river. Lumber and wheat are its major exports, and it is not unusual to see Japanese seamen snapping pictures of Simon Benson's fountains while waiting for their ship to be loaded.

The Bonneville Dam, some forty miles upstream on the Columbia, provides yet another reminder of the vital tie between the region and the river. Bonneville is one of 11 hydroelectric dams that cinch the river's mainstem below the Canadian border. During recent low-water years the power output from those dams, massive as it is, barely met the Northwest's growing demands. The struggle between citizens' groups and industry for what little power remains to be developed from the Columbia is already under way.

"We've probably developed the river to its fullest extent," Al Ramirez, the Army Corps of Engineers' projects coordinator for the Columbia, told me. "Now we have power competing with irrigation, fishing, and navigation when there is a shortage of water. We're going to have to look somewhere else in the future for energy."

A different view of the Columbia, into its ancient past, came from Portland State University geologist John Eliot Allen. John led me on a geologic tour one day through the spectacular Columbia Gorge, where the river cuts a deep passage through the Cascade Range. Near the town of The Dalles, at the eastern end of the gorge, we watched the Columbia 700 feet below us as it wound lazily between crumbling basalt cliffs.

Toward the end of the last Ice Age, John said, a great glacial lake backed up 500 cubic miles of water behind a 3,000-foot-high wall of ice near the Idaho-Montana border. When the dam broke (it may have formed and collapsed as many as 40 times during thousands of years), the flood that rushed down the Columbia was ten times the combined flow of all the world's rivers today.

"That was a flood I would like to have seen," my companion exclaimed, from the safety of geologic hindsight. "The water was 200 feet deep right over the place where we are standing."

In a fascinating geologic guide to the gorge called *The Magnificent Gateway,* John has calculated the energy of one of the Ice Age floods that swept by here. It would equal the force of a 20-kiloton nuclear bomb going off every four seconds for 10 days, he estimates, or 191 times the energy released during the 1906 San Francisco earthquake.

Those roaring floods deepened and widened the 75-mile-long canyon through the ancient lava flows of the Cascades, "A victory," in the words of my geologist friend, "of water over fire." From the old two-lane Columbia River Scenic Highway we watched that elemental struggle continuing high along the walls of the gorge. Dozens of waterfalls hurtled down misty clefts, disappearing into thick shrouds of fern and moss.

The free-flowing Columbia foamed with rapids here, a traditional fishing ground for Indians of the region. There is still some fishing for salmon, trout, and sturgeon, with nets, fishing rods, and set lines, but the great river is placid now, its rapids submerged behind the Bonneville Dam. Along the Washington side of the Columbia, camas, lupine, and other wild flowers face the sun and stain the open fields with color, while beneath the steep, shadowed cliffs on the Oregon side tourists spread picnic lunches, hardly mindful that nature once unleashed a mighty display of fury where they lounge.

I paused a few days later to watch another group of scientists attempt to harness

One of three plants being built here by a consortium of regional utilities, this project has a target date of 1984 to start producing electricity. Each plant could supply a city of half a million, but design changes, labor disputes, and cost overruns threaten the program.

the region's energy resources. This group was trying to harness the wind.

On a high bluff above the river at Good-noe Hills, east of Goldendale, Washington, engineers and craftsmen of federal agencies and the Boeing Company have constructed the world's first utility-size windmill farm. Three huge pylons, each supporting a 300-foot rotor, sat waiting for the wind to blow. A platform full of politicians and corporate dignitaries made speeches to a crowd of about a thousand people fanning themselves under the hot sun.

Windmills of this sort, explained BPA engineer Ron Holeman, need a lot of wind, about 14 miles an hour just to begin producing power. Under ideal conditions the three Goodnoe Hills windmills will generate a total of 7.5 megawatts, enough energy to light up nearby Goldendale, a town of about 3,500. Someday, Ron predicted, thousands of similar windmill clusters may be scattered across the Northwest, producing as much as 10 percent of its energy.

But the wind was playing fickle with this group. Though the rhetoric on the platform took wing, those three giant windmills stood motionless against the sky.

In 1881, Lt. Thomas Symons of the Army Corps of Engineers led a small survey party down the Columbia, riding the river in a big, flat-bottomed bateau. The lieutenant's bleak observation, when he reached the portion of the river where Richland, Washington, now stands, was that it was "an almost waterless, lifeless region . . . a desolation where even the most hopeful can find nothing in its future prospects to cheer."

With the introduction of irrigation here around the turn of this century came farming and settlers. Until World War II the farming hamlet of Richland maintained a population of some 250.

Were he to visit this area today, Lieutenant Symons would scarcely believe his eyes. Richland is a tidy community of about 34,000 with deep, green lawns and rush-hour traffic jams. This startling development in the midst of near-desert conditions is due to two crucial elements: the Columbia and the atom.

"Along the Washington side of the Columbia, camas, lupine, and other wild flowers face the sun and stain the open fields with color, while beneath the steep, shadowed cliffs on the Oregon side tourists spread picnic lunches, hardly mindful that nature once unleashed a mighty display of fury where they lounge."

The remoteness of the region and the plentiful supply of Columbia water brought the federal government here in 1943 to transform 570 square miles of scrubland into the Hanford nuclear reservation. It has given Richland and its sister cities, Pasco and Kennewick—the Tri-Cities, as they call themselves—their main source of livelihood.

At the time the reservation was established, its sole purpose was to help harness the killing power of the atom. Plutonium for an atomic bomb was produced here, in deep secrecy. The bomb eventually leveled Nagasaki, Japan, in one of the closing chapters of World War II.

By the 1950s, eight reactors—tall, gray, windowless concrete slabs—were lined up along the Columbia, turning out plutonium. Shut and empty now, except for legions of bats hanging in the dark inside, they sit like tombstones along the river.

But the Hanford Site is still a busy place. A lone remaining reactor turns out plutonium for weapons and energy research, and steam for a generating plant. Three more nuclear

"On the river is Grand Coulee Dam,/The mightiest thing ever built by a man/To run the great factories and water the land," sang balladeer Woody Guthrie. This Depression era project employed thousands of people to build a structure larger than the Great Pyramid of Egypt. Its spillway bulks above the town of Coulee Dam. A third powerhouse, now in the works, will make Grand Coulee the world's largest producer of hydroelectricity.

plants for electric power were planned for the site. One federal study in 1978 estimated that 20 or more nuclear plants could be accommodated someday at Hanford.

Richland bills itself as "The Atomic City." Its high school teams are nicknamed "The Bombers." A mild spot of radioactivity can still be detected here and there in the Columbia, a legacy of the old days when the reactors flushed their cooling water into the river—though federal officials say the levels of concentration are within established standards for drinking water. Several years ago geologists discovered young earth faults within 40 miles to the southeast and trending toward Hanford. Such faults, according to a scientist in the United States Geological Survey, suggest the possibility of renewed earth movement in the future.

The overall picture, I thought, might make some people in the post-Three Mile Island society a little nervous—and it does. There are voices raised on both sides here over the complex question of safety. The nuclear reservation at Hanford means 20,000 jobs to the Tri-Cities.

At Prosser, some 25 miles from Richland, I visited the "atomic man"—Harold "Mac" McCluskey. He was sprayed by radioactive waste in 1976 during an accident at Hanford. He was "hot" with radioactivity when they took him to the Emergency Decontamination Facility in Richland; doctors treating him wore protective suits. Mac spent three months in an area specially set up for him. He showed me where workmen had removed floor tiles after a test revealed that they had become contaminated.

One scientist calculated that Mac received 500 times the established limit of radioactivity for nuclear workers. He has since developed cataracts and other ailments, though doctors are not certain what caused

them. But the fact that he is alive at all makes Mac McCluskey something of a nuclear-age miracle man to doctors around the world.

A few days after I left Richland I read the headline bannered across a 1936 front page of the *Wenatchee Daily World* that was hanging in a frame on my motel room wall. "TWO MILLION WILD HORSES!" it screamed, in end-of-the-world type.

World publisher Rufus Woods, never one to underplay his enthusiasms (he once left his paper to join a circus passing through Wenatchee), was simply telling his readers in his own way that a dam on the Columbia at Grand Coulee, which he had first proposed in 1918, would harness two million horsepower flowing unused down the river.

After 23 years and a Presidential blessing from Franklin Delano Roosevelt, the Wenatchee publisher's dream became reality. Since it began generating power in 1941, the Grand Coulee Dam has far surpassed that newspaper prophecy. With the Grand Coulee's third powerhouse—nearing completion when I visited the site—the dam's 24 generators will be turning out 6,150 megawatts of electricity, according to operations manager Jerry Pederson. The Grand Coulee Dam will be generating enough electricity to supply the entire Seattle metropolitan area.

Pederson and I sat one afternoon in his office overlooking the Grand Coulee's massive spillway. A single penstock channeling water to a turbine in the new powerhouse, he told me, can divert more of the Columbia than all the water flowing down the Colorado River at Hoover Dam. The total capacity of all 24 penstocks could raise the river level 20 feet. Ironically, noted Pederson, the real danger downstream is large reductions in flow, which increase the potential for landslides.

The looming presence of the dam dominates the town of Coulee Dam just below. An

annual running race uses the mile-long top of the dam as part of the course. Skittish motel guests staying beside the dam's 550-foot-high face have been so unnerved by all that concrete and pent-up water that they have bolted for higher ground. The dam may even produce its own weather; sheets of water tumbling down the spillway act as a natural air conditioner. Travelers arriving here after sweltering through the desert heat of central Washington have been pleasantly surprised by the sight of people in sweaters.

Fred and Barbara Meyer live as close to the dam as you can get in Coulee Dam. They've seen rainbows from spillway spray arch across their yard. "You get used to the sound of the water coming over the dam," Fred told me. "There is one odd thing though. When the dam stops spilling water in the middle of the night, the silence wakes you up."

> *Roll along, Columbia,*
> *you can roll down to the sea,*
> *But river while you're rambling*
> *you can do some work for me.*

Woody Guthrie, America's Depression era balladeer, wrote those words about the Grand Coulee Dam and the Herculean changes it brought to this empty land. But I have never read much about the people the Grand Coulee Dam threw *out* of work.

Lost beneath the waters of Roosevelt Lake, which backs up more than 130 miles from the Grand Coulee Dam almost to the Canadian border, are thousands of acres of apple and cherry orchards and the tiny towns that serviced them. As I drove north along the narrow man-made lake, the land began to change again beside this final hidden stretch of the Columbia. The emptiness of the desert scabland—the cracked and crusted surface left behind by the glaciers and their floods here—gave way to stands of ponderosa pine

and rising foothills. But until I met Mary Gifford there was no trace of the bustling river life that once flourished here.

"Gifford was a pretty busy place before the dam," Mary Gifford said, as we thumbed through her scrapbooks. Her husband's grandfather, James O. Gifford, a one-legged Civil War veteran, started the town on the upper Columbia after he arrived here in 1889. "There was a ferry and fishing, and lots of orchards," Mary said. "Then they put up a WPA camp and 3,000 men came and just cleared the orchards and everything else out of the way for the lake."

About all that's left of the old town of Gifford is Mary's white frame house, set back off the road in a clump of pines. There's a tiny post office she runs from her kitchen and a general store next door, its red paint fading. The rest of Gifford, the dusty, dirt streets piled with crates of fruit, the hardware store, pool parlor, blacksmith shop, Odd Fellows hall . . . all lie submerged in the rippling blue stillness of Roosevelt Lake.

"I suppose Gifford is gone for good," Mary sighed, shutting the last scrapbook. "I know it's progress, but it still bothers me that no one even noticed we were here first."

I found Joe McNamee at the north end of Roosevelt Lake on a tiny free-flowing stretch of the Columbia some ten miles from the border. He invited me aboard a small dredge anchored below the town of Northport. I watched, captivated, as he swirled a slurry of water and dark sand in a pan and held it up to show me a rim of tiny, shining flecks.

"That's it," Joe said with a broad smile. "That's what we're after here—gold."

Local gossip in Northport has it that Joe and his crew of divers on the dredge have taken as much as five ounces of gold in one day from the rocky bars along the Columbia. When I asked him about this, his expression

was suddenly as blank as the gray water flowing past us. All he would say was that four more dredges were coming soon to work the riverbank he and his partners have leased as far as the border.

But Joe's silence didn't bother me. It was still a fine spring day; the snowy peaks of the Selkirk Mountains in Canada cut a ragged line against a northern sky of the deepest blue.

Somewhere up in those mountains, I'm certain, lies the mother lode, with the Columbia taking just enough of its riches to tantalize the dreamers. I hope they never find that lode. It would spoil the tension, the almost physical attraction that can grow between man and the river. And just as men are entitled to their dreams, a river like this should be allowed to keep secrets of its own forever.

Sunrise highlights peaks of Idaho's Sawtooth Range, a 41-mile-long arm of the northern Rockies. Forbidding terrain, aptly named, and bitter winters—10 months of snow, temperatures that plunge to 50 below—help preserve more than 200,000 acres in the range's Sawtooth Wilderness.

The Rockies

By Bill Richards

I wanted to see what Hemingway saw, to understand the peace he found in these high and lonely northern mountains. He never wrote a word about them in any book, although the writing desk at his home in Ketchum, Idaho, faced north toward the Sawtooths, as powerful and beautiful a mountain range as can be found anywhere.

Instead I discovered what I was seeking in a eulogy written by Hemingway for a companion killed in a hunting accident. Part of it is chiseled into a small stone memorial outside Ketchum that was erected to the author after he killed himself in 1961. An alder grove, bare in the deep February snow, gave the site a sense of solitude as I read the words.

> Best of all he loved the fall
> The leaves yellow on the cottonwoods
> Leaves floating on the trout streams
> And above the hills
> The high blue windless skies . . .
> Now he will be part of them forever.

It is gentle and personal, written in the spirit people seem to find in this awe-inspiring country. A man who has lived his life in these mountains tried to explain that feeling to me. "You can't help being humbled," he concluded. "There's so few of us and so much of them."

There is a prideful school of thought here which holds that if the mountains of Idaho were ironed flat Texans would be humbled. I can't say I subscribe to that, not that Texas can't use humility, but because these mountains fill a number of needs—playground, livelihood, and perhaps most of all, refuge.

Wintertime can make the northern Rockies remote and forbidding to an outsider like me. But traveling along the mountain rim of the Northwest in Idaho and Montana I found small towns bursting with activity under their heavy mantle of snow, their inhabitants seeming to enjoy a winter that lasts half the year. Far from isolating people, the mountains seem to add to the quality of companionship here—people don't just talk to each other, they "visit." The T-shirt I came across in northern Idaho summed things up nicely.

"Idaho is," it said, "what America was."

Ninety-nine mountain ranges lace this state. Many of them, along with the mountains of northwest Montana and a bit of eastern Washington, make up the Idaho Batholith. It covers nearly 25,000 square miles. Batholith is Greek for "deep stone." No one has plumbed the floor of this one, the largest batholith in the contiguous United States, and the matter is one of controversy.

Professor George Williams, head of the geology department at the University of Idaho, explained to me that one group of geologists believes the batholith here is really a mammoth chunk of igneous rock sitting on top of other rock many miles beneath the earth's surface. Another of the theories says the batholith is a magma mass with no real bottom; it worked its way to the earth's surface around 100 million years ago, and has been gradually uncovered by erosion. "I guess that argument will be going a long time," Williams said.

I was still pondering a debate in which millions of years could be tossed around so casually as I sat a few nights later in the midst of the mountains, up to my chin in hot water. A bath in a horse trough, heated by a wood-burning boiler, is a welcome, if unusual, reward after a day of plodding 7,000-foot-high ridges on cross-country skis. My aches melted away in the tub. The mountains loomed against a sky black as an inkwell as I wrapped a towel around myself and strolled, still steaming, through the snow to the tent.

"I built that contraption for myself. After a few days up here you need to be good to

The northern Rockies: natural treasure and national playground on the eastern rim of the Northwest. Pacific winds, which leave little moisture in the desert lands, rise and cool at this lofty barrier; down comes the powder skiers crave. From storied Silver Valley to booming Challis, miners wrest ore from the uplands. In Montana sheep and cattle summer in alpine pastures and winter in sheltered valleys. Glacier National Park, the Sawtooths, and other remote strongholds embrace millions of unspoiled acres in spectacular settings.

yourself," said Joe Leonard. Joe, a 42-year-old professional guide, and his helper Steve Mahan were leading our party of five skiers through the 754,000-acre Sawtooth National Recreation Area. We had started in Stanley.

For those who can muster the energy and master a few skills, this kind of ski touring is a happy escape from the lift lines and crowded downhill trails at the resorts. Joe and Steve let loose with whoops as they flew down a hillside unbroken by a single track. The rest of us followed in clumsy imitation; the hill was soon marred with the evidence of our tumbles. "You have to want a little adventure and be willing to pay the price of some physical effort," Joe said later. "But it's so much fun I feel guilty taking money for it."

South of this rugged country, some 50 miles away, lies Sun Valley, an incongruous dollop of pseudo-Tyrol with a worldwide reputation among downhill skiers. It is hard not to smile at a resort whose location was picked out by an imported Austrian count, and whose inn was built to the specifications of a movie-set designer from California.

Averell Harriman ordered the construction of Sun Valley in 1936. One story goes that Harriman wanted to build up long-distance ridership for his Union Pacific Railroad. But as he remembers it, he and Mrs. Harriman had become enchanted with the ski towns in the Alps and wanted to duplicate one over here. Through the years some of the frills have disappeared. No longer, for instance, are four staff members assigned to each guest, and the dogsled team that used to meet the Union Pacific train is gone—as, alas, is the train itself.

Still, I found it a bit startling when I walked into a restaurant for a hamburger and discovered a man strumming background music on an electric zither. And my Austrian ski instructor woke me up abruptly during

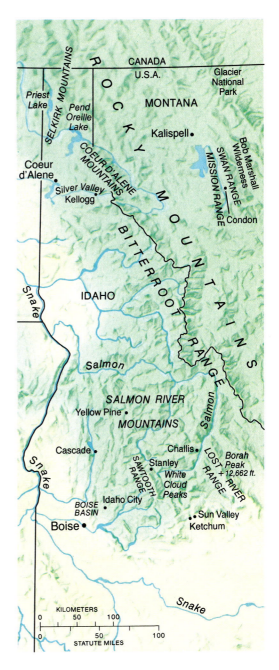

Snow-draped sentries, giant fir and spruce trees surround a skier tracking cross country in the Selkirk Mountains of Idaho's panhandle, a year-round center for outdoor sport. Skiers, many from nearby Canada, head for Schweitzer Basin; campers, hikers, and fishermen resort to forested trails and three huge lakes—Priest, Pend Oreille, and Coeur d'Alene.

one of our morning rides up a ski lift when he suddenly burst out yodeling.

"Sun Valley has always been itself," said Dorice Taylor. Still a winter sports enthusiast at 79, Mrs. Taylor joined me after finishing a round of cross-country skiing on Sun Valley's golf course. She and her lawyer husband, Everett "Phez" Taylor, have lived at Sun Valley since they quit New York City in 1940. For nearly 25 years, as head of the resort's publicity department, she logged the comings and goings of the rich and famous. The names tumble out of Mrs. Taylor's memory bank—DuPonts, Fords, Harrimans, Kennedys, Clark Gable, Ingrid Bergman, Gary Cooper, foreign potentates with their own chefs, industrialists with their own railroad cars.

"The movie studios all used to have batches of starlets they'd send up here from Hollywood to have their pictures taken on the ski slopes," Mrs. Taylor recalled. "We'd get them and run them through the publicity mill of course. But I'm afraid a lot of those girls never did get to know a pair of skis from a swizzle stick."

Times have changed. Sun Valley still gets its share of the rich and famous. But movie stars tend to look like everybody else now in designer jeans and sunglasses. And nobody wants a picture taken any more, I was told, for fear of alerting burglars back home that a house stands empty.

Tourism and outdoor sports are booming in the northern Rockies. In Idaho alone they comprise an industry that has reached 800 million dollars a year. But such growth is a fairly recent phenomenon. Scratch a slope covered with schussers from Texas and California and you are likely to uncover history related to what lies beneath the mountains, not on top of them.

Nearly 120 years ago Bannock, today known as Idaho City, to the west of the Sawtooths, lay at the center of another kind of boom. Thousands of men—miners, clerks, dreamers, and gamblers—rushed into these hills looking for their share of the gold discovered in 1862 in the Boise Basin.

Instant boomtowns rose; some dissolved just as quickly. A rumor, a knowing look, or a sudden departure in the middle of the night was often enough to start a stampede. In such a charged atmosphere violence often prevailed. A newspaper in 1870 noted that many murders had taken place in the Territory in the previous seven years, but only a few killers ever stood trial.

Among the tents and brick and wooden buildings that made up Idaho City in those days were 39 saloons, said John Brogan. As mayor of present-day Idaho City—population 300—John presides over a town that is only a husk of its former self. His grandfather, James McDevitt, a San Francisco butcher afflicted with wanderlust, joined the gold rush east into Idaho in 1863 from California's worked-out claims. The bonanza placer strikes in the Boise Basin didn't last long either. Many were abandoned within seven years of McDevitt's arrival. But the boom lasted just long enough for Idaho City to make the history books as the most populous town in the entire Pacific Northwest—for a couple of years.

Among the toughest of the men who made their way into Idaho's mountains were the government mail carriers. Equipped with snowshoes and with skis that measured up to 11 feet, these pioneers crossed passes thousands of feet high to bring the mail to snowbound miners' camps a century ago. It was hazardous work and some never made it. Along one route in the Boise River country, three carriers were crushed by avalanches in the 1880s. Another was found frozen to death on the same trail, his pack crammed with Christmas mail. *(Continued on page 182)*

Etched deep in a Rocky Mountain basin, Sun Valley caters to skiers from around the world. At sunrise a patroller on Bald Mountain radios snow conditions to the lodge; soon up to a dozen lifts will begin to whir, hauling 17,000 skiers an hour at peak load. The world's first chair lift

opened here in 1936. Fabled downhill runs—"Baldy" has attracted world-class racers—and the resort's cosmopolitan style make for soaring real estate prices; a home in the village may sell for a million dollars. The Rockies also offer simpler joys: A cross-country skier eases his aches in a horse trough doing service as a wilderness hot tub.

FOLLOWING PAGES: *Even flying demands skis when snow cover on mountain strips exceeds six inches. Ray Arnold pilots a Cessna that serves as post office, ambulance, and taxi along roadless miles of the Salmon River country.*

Mail call at Yellowpine Bar on the Main Salmon River brings Val Richardson and "Newt" Haigh to the airstrip. Pilot Ray Arnold (in plaid shirt) also delivers supplies and news, by word of mouth, as he covers this route once a week. Another customer, journalist Frances Wisner of Campbell's Ferry (below left), salutes the Idaho backcountry: "I never tire of it. I've been here 40 years and see something new every day." Arnold banks steeply amid thickly forested summits for one of 13 landings on the Main Salmon route. He prefers to fly only in good

weather; maneuvering in
the mountains proves
difficult, and local fields
lack instruments. In winter
his precious deliveries
arrive only twice a month.

Ray Arnold continues that rugged tradition. Ray, a 43-year-old pilot in Cascade, Idaho, flies freight and passengers, and runs the Salmon River Air Star Route, the only one of its kind in the contiguous United States. The government pays him $18,000 a year to deliver mail to about a hundred customers; to my mind it is money well earned.

On the first and third Wednesday of each month through the winter, weather permitting, Ray climbs into his red-and-white Cessna, waves goodbye to his wife, Carol, and flies off into the backcountry of the Salmon River Mountains. His 300-mile mail route covers some of the most isolated country in America. When someone asks Ray if he can land in a crosswind between granite cliffs on a rumpled cow pasture not much longer than a suburban driveway, he is likely to smile and say, "You can bet your life on it."

The day I flew with Ray I learned a new dimension to a job I had always taken for granted. In addition to the mail, groceries, and a young woman named Nancy Schrock and her German shepherd, Chevak, I was crammed into the Cessna 206 along with 30 cases of beer. Carol Arnold casually asked how much I weighed, then began fiddling with her calculator to figure the total weight.

Ray estimates he has logged 30,000 takeoffs and landings in nine years of flying the backcountry. We made only 20 on our trip, but each produced a bit of suspense: a canyon wall topped at just the right spot; a tall pine cut so close on an approach that I could count the cones; a landing strip that would be too short except that we landed heading up a 20-degree grade. Suddenly we were flying down a box canyon very low, so low in fact that I began searching nervously along the stream below for a flat place to set down.

"There's a herd of mountain goats somewhere around here I thought you might like to see," Ray yelled as he scanned the shadowy walls closing in around us. He had been here many times before and I ought to have been reassured, but I was not. The goats, when we found them, were perched on a ledge *above* our plane.

More than a mailman, Ray is a lifeline for the people who stay through the winter to watch over the dude ranches and other way stations along the Salmon River and its wilderness tributaries. During the summer and fall as many as 16,000 rafters, as well as hunters and hikers, come through here, but in winter it is a cold, lonely place. Ray has performed night rescue missions through the area, flying, he says with a grin, "by touch." The Cessna hauls everything from llamas—used as pack animals at a dude ranch—to cigarettes for Frances Wisner. We land on the strip at her Campbell's Ferry homestead, and I shut my eyes as Ray whips the little plane around at the end of the runway. The pine forest starts just a few feet beyond.

There is a bond of admiration and trust between Ray and his customers. They bake cookies for him and turn over blank checks he fills in later for their grocery orders. He passes on a little gossip from the outside over coffee. "If it wasn't for Ray," a woman confided, as I helped unload houseplants for her remote cabin, "none of us would be here."

"It takes a special kind of person to live out here," Ray said. "If you can't make do,

*Stetson and six-gun suggest two of Terry Rekow's trades—cowboy and ranch manager
in the Salmon River Mountains. He needs more than two skills, for Yellow Pine, his home,
has only 50 full-time residents. Rekow also works as a guide, saddler, and surveyor's aide.*

sometimes there's no alternative. Break a leg in a storm and you just have to tough it out."

Before we finished the route, the western sky was streaked with deep purple and orange; shadows swallowed all but the mountaintops. We flew 65 miles toward home without seeing a light below, until Ray radioed Carol that he was coming in. The Cessna banked; suddenly a warm light shone from a small hangar—and Idaho's flying mailman was home.

Deep in mountain-locked forests, I came upon Yellow Pine, a tiny community cut off by snowed-in passes from the rest of central Idaho for as long as five months of the year. There really isn't much size to the town—a few bars, a one-room schoolhouse, a handful of buildings tucked into a valley—but I found it hard to tell exactly how many people live there. Yellow Pine may be secluded, but the pace can get hectic.

On the day I flew in I found a chess tournament going and the playoffs for the annual pool championships under way. A snowmobile club had come some 50 miles from McCall, after crossing Lick Creek Summit, 6,879 feet high. Nearly everyone in town ate through a Chinese potluck supper, then crossed the street and crowded into Buck and Faye Stark's cafe and saloon to dance to the music of the Johnson Creek Band (accordion, piano, and washboard bass).

I finally managed to count 50 or so residents of this busy little wilderness oasis. During World War II, Yellow Pine felt the ripples of a brief boom while more than a thousand miners worked in the surrounding mountains. Tungsten and nearly 95 percent of the antimony used by the United States in the war came from this area and went into making storage batteries and the paint used on warships. After the war the miners left, and the people of Yellow Pine—a few trappers,

outfitters, retirees, and assorted drifters—settled down to ignore, and be ignored by, the rest of the world.

People here seem to like it that way. There is only one television set in town, with awful reception. There is no telephone service, although the local CB radio net buzzes throughout the day. Perhaps because of its enforced isolation, separate strands of society—young and old, redneck and longhair—are knit together. "Yellow Pine is unique," Don Waller explained over a beer one day. "People accept each other for what they are; nobody pushes. This is like a town that existed a hundred years ago."

Waller is a strapping man of 30, an Idaho native who occasionally dresses in homemade buckskins and who makes his living as a trapper and hunting guide. When things get quiet in Yellow Pine he sometimes dreams out loud about what life must have been like for the early mountain pioneers. Two years ago he decided to live out one of his fantasies. He hitched a team of horses to a heavy freight sleigh in Yellow Pine and set out to drive the rig over the mountains to Cascade, just the way the mountain men used to do. The temperature plunged way below zero and the round trip took five days. When he arrived back here, his beard covered with ice, the whole town turned out to cheer. "Sometimes it isn't easy getting along with everyone," said Don Millen, a retired Californian, "and it can be even harder learning to get along with yourself. If a person's going to like this country, he finds out the first winter."

A few days later I discovered another type of learning experience taking place when I arrived in Challis, Idaho. Until recently, Challis might have been any one of hundreds of small, dusty, western towns sleeping away the years amid spectacular mountains—the Lost River Range, the Salmons,

Snowbound folk of Yellow Pine look to indoor diversions to enliven the long winters. The chess games in the Corner Bar prove more popular than pinball; in the one-room elementary school, one-fourth of the student body hits the books. When they reach high-school age, students continue with correspondence courses or board out of town.
FOLLOWING PAGES: *Center stage on Saturday night, the three-piece Johnson Creek Band rocks Buck and Faye's cafe in Yellow Pine. Visiting snowmobilers often jam the session.*

and the White Clouds—without traffic lights, without a shopping center, and with one bank handling all the business between Challis and its nearest sizable neighbor, Salmon, nearly 60 miles to the north.

But late in 1979 the Cyprus Mines Corporation, a worldwide minerals company, announced that it was going to mine molybdenum at a site 31 road miles from here. The Cyprus operation would entail a mill and a mile-wide open-pit mine. Other companies were also exploring for molybdenum as well as tungsten, fluorspar, uranium, gold, and silver in the mountains nearby. Things have been changing in a hurry in Challis.

The headline on the newspaper I bought at the local pharmacy carried this plaintive appeal: "Challis Officials Ask Job Seekers to Stay Away for Time Being." Cyprus company policy called for hiring local people first— part of an elaborate and expensive campaign to demonstrate its corporate good citizenship. Yet the town was jammed. It took me two trips up and down the main street to find a parking spot; by noon every motel in town

had lit its "No Vacancy" sign. Clusters of vehicle campers with out-of-town plates huddled in open fields. State health officials were on the scene investigating an outbreak of hepatitis at a crowded trailer camp some 30 miles outside of town. The population of Challis, about 1,000, was expected to increase by 50 percent by 1983, when Cyprus planned to begin operating its mine.

Though the company challenges the view and has sought to avoid runaway growth, it seemed to me that Challis was taking its place alongside other overloaded communities such as Gillette, Wyoming, and Colstrip, Montana, as another stop on the sad circuit of western mineral boomtowns.

People have much to say for and against what is happening in these places. The arguments usually come down to pitting jobs and resource needs against environment and an old-fashioned quality of life. Both sides can score endless debating points, but they usually don't change the course of development after it gathers momentum. I left town and spent the afternoon in *(Continued on page 190)*

Bleak slopes blight the landscape around the Bunker Hill Company lead smelter in Kellogg, Idaho. Forest fires in the early 1900s ravaged these bluffs; sulfur dioxide released during smelting acidified the soil, preventing regrowth. The company sought to green the hills by nursing seedlings in a mine (right) with artificial sunlight and air rich in carbon dioxide. Low mineral prices in 1981 led Bunker Hill to announce plans to close. But mining still molds the environment and the economy here in Silver Valley, accounting for 40 percent of U. S. silver production. Collector's coins honor the area's richest lode, the Sunshine Mine.

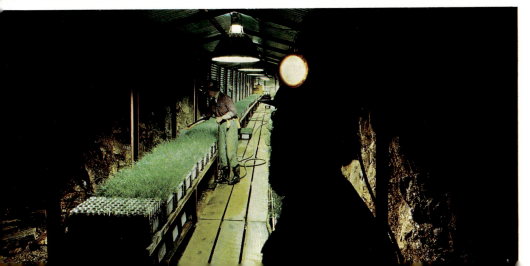

the nearby hills to get an idea of what the first mountain men and trappers saw when they pushed into the Salmon River country in the 1820s. These early adventurers included the Hudson's Bay Company's intrepid explorer Alexander Ross, and mountain men Jedediah Smith and Jim Bridger, all as wild in their way as the country they roamed searching for beaver, otter, and muskrat.

From where I sat I could see the snowy tips of the Lost River Range to the east as they turned gold and then lavender in the late afternoon sun. The Salmon, given the haunting name "River of No Return" by pioneers who could travel only downstream on its swift, treacherous waters, seemed only a trickle; distant clouds hid Borah Peak, at 12,662 feet Idaho's highest mountain.

I saw no sign of the herds of pronghorn, elk, and mountain goats that roam here, but plenty of deer and bighorn sheep tracks crisscrossed my hill.

Given the finite limits of the mountain wilderness left today, it is easy to romanticize those trappers who passed through, barely leaving their mark, and condemn the miners, whose mark is only too evident on the land. But the history of the northern Rockies is, for the most part, a mining history. Miners settled much of this region, and its heritage is usually their own.

Nowhere is that heritage more evident than in Idaho's Silver Valley. Interstate 90 picks its way across the northern panhandle here, through twisting canyons made ugly by silver-mine tailings spilling off the mountainsides and a mile-long slag heap from the giant lead smelter serving the Bunker Hill Company mines at Kellogg. The company's announcement in 1981 that market conditions would force it to close down its Kellogg operations sent tremors through the valley. Some 2,100 jobs were at stake.

The agony of this landscape hides its beauty, deep beneath the surface. There, long veins of silver are shot through fractures in brittle quartzite. The immense lode results from deep-seated geologic processes found nowhere else, as far as geologists have been able to determine. It is estimated that the tunnels dug in the Coeur d'Alene Mountains here would stretch from Boston to Washington, D. C., and the digging continues.

The boom began in 1885, one story goes, with Noah Kellogg's jackass. Noah, a drifter following the gold stampeders through the Northwest, was prospecting here when the jackass wandered off. Noah stooped to grab a rock to toss at the beast. The rock was heavy and Noah, hoping as much as suspecting that he had something more than ammunition, carried it to an assayer.

The story should end there with Kellogg becoming one of the first in a long string of mining millionaires from the Coeur d'Alene region. But it didn't. Noah ran through his riches and died broke. Kellogg, the gritty smelter town which bears his name, put up a sign to commemorate its antecedents. "You are now near KELLOGG," it said. "The Town which was discovered by a JACKASS—and which is inhabited by its Descendants."

A mile below ground in the Sunshine Mine just east of Kellogg, Glen Caldwell, his face streaked with dirt and sweat under his hardhat, pointed to a dark smudge on the ceiling. "That vein," he told me, "runs nearly 60 feet long and it's just about solid silver. We've been working this part of the mine for 13 years and just found it. You never know when you're gonna hit."

Nearly a billion ounces of silver have been recovered from the Coeur d'Alenes, about 300 million ounces from the Sunshine Mine alone, making it the biggest silver producer in the country. The silver taken from this 30-mile-long valley since the beginning of the century, when refined to 99.9 percent purity, would fill two mile-long freight trains of 50-ton cars.

The cost of these riches in human lives has been heavy. In 1972 a fire at the Sunshine Mine killed 91 men, the worst hardrock mining disaster since 1917. Hardrock miners here, as elsewhere, suffer and die from silicosis—"dust on the lung" they call it. A week before my tour a miner died when 50 feet of rock and muck collapsed on top of him.

Some people measure the riches of the mountains not in gold or silver but in moments of unbroken silence, breaths of clean, cold air on a summit, or even—as in the case of two unusual doctors I met in Kalispell, Montana—in pawprints in the snow. Rusby Seabaugh and Jim McCreedy chase mountain lions and bobcats in their spare time with the sort of fervor many of their colleagues reserve for golf or tennis. To these two nothing could be more satisfying than 170 pounds of skittish mountain lion lodged in a tree after a chase through the mountains. When they are not busy with patients, Rusby and Jim are usually high on some ridgeline in the snows of the Swan or Mission mountains of northwest Montana, tracking behind a pair of noisy hunting hounds named Ed and Tom.

"We tree cats, we don't kill them," Rusby explains on a clear morning as we make our way into the Swans. Ed and Tom shuffle and whine impatiently in the back of Rusby's mud-spattered pickup. "The chase is the skill," says Rusby. "Once you've got a cat in a tree you've caught him. There isn't much sport in killing him."

Instead, Jim will usually shinny up after a treed mountain lion and tranquilize it with a dart. When the groggy cat staggers down the tree a few minutes later, the doctors tattoo it in the ear and place an identification collar

Signs of the times: Hardhat facade and a modified town marker reflect Idaho's reliance on mining. A neon lamp flickers on as a real estate man lowers the flag at his Kellogg office. Spurred by plans for a new molybdenum mine near Challis, pranksters multiplied the population by ten. Whimsy exaggerates, but hundreds of job-seekers crowded in.

on its neck. The markers help state authorities keep track of the number of cats roaming through the wilderness.

It can be a tricky sport. A bobcat may cross and recross its trail a dozen times to throw pursuing dogs off its scent. A mountain lion may roam up to 20 miles in a day. Our conversation has swung to politics when Rusby slams the pickup to a halt and jumps out to inspect a set of small tracks in the fresh snow. "Bobcat," he says and drops the tailgate. Ed and Tom topple out, falling over each other in their enthusiasm, and are off in a flash into the thick fir and pine.

A good hunting dog will pick up the direction a cat is heading from a fresh track. We move up the ridge behind the dogs, zigzagging with the bobcat's trail. An hour later I am

"After a few more miles of this, the dogs are running in circles and we are bumping into each other. We scan the treetops hopefully, but there is no sign of a bobcat. We have lost him. Three trackers and two trained dogs versus one small, running bobcat. In the mountains the odds are not always what they seem."

wet from pushing through the snowy pines and winded from the climb. The cat—or cats; the trail seems to be doubling back and forth across itself—has not picked the easy route. The dogs howl—enthusiasts of the chase call it "hound music"—but they are coming back down the mountain toward us.

"That cat ain't caught yet," announces Jim McCreedy. Indeed. After a few more miles of this, the dogs are running in circles and we are bumping into each other. We scan the treetops hopefully, but there is no sign of a bobcat. We have lost him. Three trackers and two trained dogs versus one small, running bobcat. In the mountains the odds are not always what they seem.

More than 40 years ago a traveler in the Swan River Valley filed this report for the Federal Writers' Project guide to Montana: "A wild land with fish and game, rude trails, and lookout stations. . . . The forest silence is broken only by the calls of wild things, the splash and gurgle of tumbling streams, and the sound, like the surf on a far shore, of wind flowing smoothly through the tops of tamaracks and firs. Nevertheless occasional cabins beside the road indicate that a few hardy human beings attempt to live here."

Much has remained the same since that was written. "Wild things"—grizzly, moose, elk, perhaps even a wolf or two—can still be found in this part of the mountain Northwest. Beyond the Swan Range on the east side of the valley, the Bob Marshall Wilderness stretches over 1,010,000 acres. Picture a preserve half again the size of Rhode Island without a car, a grocery store, a television set, or a permanent dweller. That is the wilderness people here in the Swan River Valley refer to as "the Bob."

As in "Save the Bob," the sign I read over the counter in Paula Vinicor's tiny Swan Cafe in the Condon area. Along with creations she calls Mel-burgers and Billi-burgers, Paula, a cheery former schoolteacher from New York State, serves up Bob-burgers to travelers who pull in off Montana Route 83. Every time somebody buys a Bob-burger she tosses 25 cents into a jar under the counter and announces: "For the cause."

"I'm like a lot of people here. I came because of the wilderness," Paula said. "It's so beautiful I could spend half my day just standing at the cafe window looking at it. Now we're worried we could lose it to the energy companies." The Bob sits astride the Overthrust Belt, a vast subterranean strip of rock stretching from Utah into Canada. Energy companies have found oil and gas hidden elsewhere within the Overthrust Belt, and they would like to explore under the Bob for more. Wilderness enthusiasts have been fighting the proposed intrusion; they hailed actions by the United States Forest Service and the House of Representatives' Interior Committee which blocked oil and gas leases in the Bob. However, energy interests have challenged these actions in the courts.

The controversy might be just another environmental skirmish, but it has a particular symbolism. Bob Marshall was a Forest Service official himself, an explorer who penetrated Alaska's remote Brooks Range, and the author of early federal regulations in the 1930s that led to the expansion of national forest wilderness areas.

Over the years the Forest Service has been the butt of much criticism from environmentalists and others who question its "multiple use" policy on federal lands. There is some question to me whether allowing a mining company to strip-mine a portion of a national forest renders that land good for many other uses. But I have met Forest Service employees with a deep reverence for wilderness as it is spelled out in the landmark federal act of 1964. The act defines wilderness as "an area . . . untrammeled by man."

In a way Bud Moore fits that category of Forest Service employee. After 41 years with the Service, Bud left a management job in a regional office in Missoula, Montana, to become a trapper in the mountains around the Swan River Valley. He is the son of a trapper and logger, and he spent his youth roaming alone high in Montana's Bitterroot Range. At 63, Bud is still a tall, lean man who does not mind snowshoeing 13 miles in a day through 10-foot mountain drifts. "I decided to live the things I believed in," Bud told me over a

lunch of elk burgers Janet Moore cooked for us. "You can't manage land from behind a desk. You have to be on it to fully understand it." From the windows of the cabin Bud and Janet built for themselves near Condon, there is a fine view of mountains rising on all sides of the 80 acres of land they have named Coyote Forest.

Bud talked about the Friends of the Bob, a group fighting energy exploration in the preserve. "There is no way," he said, "that the wilderness of the Bob, or the wilderness of any place for that matter, can survive the prospecting and exploiting for gas or oil. And we intend to do all in our power to keep the wilderness in . . . the Bob Marshall country."

Later we headed up into the Mission Range, where Bud does most of his winter trapping for lynx and marten. The air around us was alive with the astringent scent of pine and cedar, and across the valley a low mountain storm spilled out of the Bob, packing the adjacent Swan mountains in a thick cotton batting of clouds.

I stood there and received the mountains' "good tidings." John Muir's words. In the mountains, he had written, peace "will flow into you as sunshine flows into trees. The winds will blow their own freshness into you, and the storms their energy."

The westering tides of American life have transformed the spacious northwest corner of our land. There is a raw and still-young triumph in the gleaming cities and the aerospace plants that rim Puget Sound, in the web of man-made waterways that have turned desert into farmland, in the newly felled forests, and in the capture of the restless Columbia. But it is good that wilderness places like this remain, places that Muir saw, that Hemingway saw, the "high blue windless skies" to remind us of the paradox of a land that is both so strong and yet so fragile.

193

Notes on Contributors

Staff photographer ROBERT W. MADDEN, who covered his first GEOGRAPHIC assignment in 1966, has developed a special interest in ethnic communities and in the problems of land use. His awards include Photographer of the Year in 1971, and Magazine Photographer of the Year and an Overseas Press Club prize for best foreign photographic coverage in 1976.

Assistant Editor ROWE FINDLEY, who joined the Society staff in 1959, was gathering material on national forests when Mount St. Helens began to rumble in 1980. He witnessed the eruption and its aftermath, and wrote memorable reports for GEOGRAPHIC. He also wrote the Special Publication *Great American Deserts.*

MARK MILLER has worked in print and broadcast journalism—and as a foreman both on a cattle ranch and an apple orchard in the Northwest. For GEOGRAPHIC he has written articles on the Yakima Valley and the Oregon coast. He was born in South Dakota, free-lances from Los Angeles.

CYNTHIA RUSS RAMSAY, a native New Yorker, treasures pockets of wilderness; she enjoyed the opportunity to explore the Northwest's distinctive mix of urban amenity and pristine landscape. Her career on the Special Publications Division staff has taken her from Alaska to Antarctica, from Sri Lanka to the Sudan, into mountaineering, archaeology, geology— "whatever's up."

BILL RICHARDS, another New Yorker, spent several years as western correspondent for the *Washington Post.* He has free-lanced articles for NATIONAL GEOGRAPHIC on the Yellowstone River and on the energy boom in the Rockies. Richards lives in Washington, D. C.

Composition for *America's Spectacular Northwest* by National Geographic's Photographic Services, Carl M. Shrader, Chief, Lawrence F. Ludwig, Assistant Chief. Printed and bound by Holladay-Tyler Printing Corp., Rockville, Md. Color separations by the Lanman Progressive Corp., Washington, D. C.; Lincoln Graphics, Inc., Cherry Hill, N.J.; N.E.C., Inc., Nashville, Tenn.

On a goodwill tour up the Columbia, the steamer tug Portland *churns by Mount Hood and the Oregon port of Hood River. Pilots long preferred the quick throttle response and maneuverability of the* Portland *for the heavy jobs in the tricky waters of her namesake port.*

Index

Boldface indicates illustrations; *italics* refer to picture legends

Acknowledgments

The Special Publications Division gratefully acknowledges the kindness of the people who welcomed the staff into their homes and work places and leisure hours and thereby immeasurably enriched this account of the Northwest. In addition we wish to thank local and federal officials and the scholars and others mentioned in the book or cited here for invaluable aid: Michael Barclay, Glenn Beckman, Bryce Breitenstein, David M. Checkley, Walter E. Conner, Gordon H. Dailey, Amos and Cally Galpin, Mary Marie Gey, Kenneth Heid, Nona Hengen, Richard M. Highsmith, Donald A. Hull, Chris Johns, Brian T. Lanker, Joe and Sheila Leonard, Vaughn E. Livingston, E. Kimbark MacColl, John Marshall, Wayne S. Moen, Ralph Perry, Donald W. Peterson, Alys R. Richmond-White, Phil Schofield, Rich Shulman, Steve Small, Michael D. Sullivan, Roy W. Van Denburgh, Beverly F. Vogt, Merle W. Wells, Doug M. Wilson; the U. S. Forest Service, the National Park Service, and the Smithsonian Institution.

The editors are also grateful for permission to reprint excerpts from "The Grand Coulee Dam," words and music by Woody Guthrie, The Richmond Organization-Copyright © 1958 and 1963 Ludlow Music, Inc., New York, N.Y.; and from "Roll On, Columbia," words by Woody Guthrie, music based on "Goodnight Irene" by Huddie Ledbetter and John Lomax, TRO-Copyright © 1936 (renewed 1964), 1957, and 1963 Ludlow Music.

Additional Reading

The issues of NATIONAL GEOGRAPHIC include numerous articles on the Northwest; consult the magazine's cumulative index. In addition, the following books proved useful in the preparation of this volume. Works that cover the region include: Otis W. Freeman and Howard H. Martin, *The Pacific Northwest*; Richard M. Highsmith and A. Jon Kimerling, eds., *Atlas of the Pacific Northwest*; David Lavender, *Land of Giants*; Bates McKee, *Cascadia: The Geologic Evolution of the Pacific Northwest*; Neal R. Peirce, *The Pacific States of America*; Gordon Speck, *Northwest Explorations*.

Other books that were helpful include volumes on the Northwest states in the American Guide Series; John Eliot Allen, *The Magnificent Gateway*; Ray Atkeson and Archie Satterfield, *Oregon Coast* and *Washington II*; Charles H. Carey, *General History of Oregon: Through Early Statehood*; William O. Douglas, *My Wilderness: The Pacific West*; Dick d'Easum, *Sawtooth Tales*; Denzel and Nancy Ferguson, *Oregon's Great Basin Country*; James A. Gibbs, *Shipwrecks of the Pacific Coast*; Stephen L. Harris, *Fire & Ice: The Cascade Volcanoes*; Stewart H. Holbrook, *The Columbia*; E. R. Jackman and R. A. Long, *The Oregon Desert*; Fred O. Jones, *Grand Coulee from "Hell to Breakfast"*; Ruth Kirk, *Exploring the Olympic Peninsula*; William L. Mainwaring, *Exploring the Oregon Coast*; Murray Morgan, *Puget's Sound*; Terence O'Donnell and Thomas Vaughan, *Portland: A Historical Sketch and Guide*; Roger Sale, *Seattle: Past to Present*; U. S. Department of Energy Bonneville Power Administration, *Multipurpose Dams of the Pacific Northwest*; Edwin Van Syckle, *They Tried To Cut It All*; Robin Will, *Beautiful Portland*.

Library of Congress Cataloging in Publication Data
Main entry under title:

America's spectacular Northwest.

   Bibliography: p.
   Includes index.
   1. Northwest, Pacific—Description and travel—1981-   —Addresses, essays, lectures. 2. Northwest, Pacific—Social life and customs—Addresses, essays, lectures. I. Madden, Robert W. II. National Geographic Society (U. S.). Special Publications Division.
F852.2.A57   979.5   80-7829
ISBN 0-87044-363-1 (regular binding)   AACR2
ISBN 0-87044-368-2 (library binding)

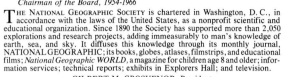